CENTRE FOR THE STUDY OF ISLAM AND OTHER FAITHS

CSIOF Bulletin

Issue No. 4
November 2011

CSIOF Bulletin

No 4. (2011)

ISSN 1836-3490
ISBN 978-0-9870793-1-2
© 2011 Melbourne School of Theology Press. All rights reserved

Editor

Peter Riddell

Assistant Editor

Kathryn Simon

Production and Cover Design

Ho-yuin Chan and Philip Brookes

Publishing Services

Published by Melbourne School of Theology Press.
Thank you to Mark Durie for publishing services.

Centre for the Study of Islam and Other Faiths

Melbourne School of Theology
5 Burwood Highway, Wantirna, Victoria 3152, Australia.
Po Box 6257 Vermont Sth, Victoria 3133, Australia
Ph: +61 3 9881 7800, Fax: +61 3 9800 0121
csiof@mst.edu.au, www.mst.edu.au

People involved in the field of Muslim-Christian relations are welcome to submit related items to the Editor for consideration for publishing in the CSIOF Bulletin.

Opinions and conclusions published in the *CSIOF Bulletin* are those of the authors and do not necessarily represent the views of the Editor or the CSIOF. The Bulletin is purely an information medium, to inform interested parties of religious trends, discussions and debates. The Bulletin does not intend in any way to actively promote hatred of any religion or its followers.

EDITORIAL	5
FEATURES	7
9/11 – Ten years on – What have we learned?	7
Engaging with a Multifaith Society: why bother?	14
A Reflective History of CRIB (1998 –)	22
British Evangelical responses to Islam: Some key findings	27
Dialogue on Social Concerns in Britain: Faith and Society (1997-2003)	33
Faith-Full Citizens: Christians and Muslims in Britain	39
Strangers in the Land	48
Legislating Against Creeping Sharia in Britain	57
Islamic Finance: For and Against	67
The Israel/ Palestine Conflict	73
Death and Dying in Hinduism and Islam	82
COMMUNIQUÉS	91
Tablighi Jama'at's Ideal Woman: Invisible and Anonymous	91
When Some Muslims Cross the Line	93
CONFERENCE REPORTS	99
Symposium: What's Happening in the Middle East	99
Symposium: Australia's Changing Demographic and its Implications for Christian-Muslim Relations	100
Muslim-Christian Forum: "Is the Qur'an the word of God?"	102
QUOTATIONS AND WRITINGS	105

REVIEWS 107

Holy Books have a HISTORY: Textual Histories
of the New Testament & the Qur'an 107
Studies on Islam and Society in Southeast Asia 110
Film Perspectives on Muhammad, from 1977 to 2011 114
Allah: A Christian Response 117
Spiders of Allah: Travels of an unbeliever on the
frontline of holy war 120
The Third Choice: Islam, Dhimmitude and Freedom 122

CSIOF NEWS AND ACTIVITIES 125

Postgraduate Research Seminars on Islam
and Related Topics 2011 125
Notes for Contributors 126

Editorial

The appearance of this 4th issue of the *CSIOF Bulletin* coincides with the 10th anniversary of the tragic 9/11 attacks in the USA. In our lead feature article, Bernie Power reflects on those attacks and subsequent events, posing a series of important questions about the present situation of the Islam-West relationship.

Christian engagement with Muslims takes many forms: evangelism, dialogue and discussions of public policy. Also presented is a series of articles that address each of these in turn, placing particular emphasis on the British and Australian contexts. Australians can learn a lot by considering today's Britain, where the Muslim community is twice as large in terms of percentages, and where the successes and challenges in the relationship between Muslims and broader society arguably provide a model for the future in Australia. Also considered in these articles are deep tensions that exist among British Christians regarding methods of engagement with Muslims; again Australian Christians can learn much in examining these tensions and drawing appropriate lessons.

The CSIOF exists to consider a broad range of non-Christian faiths. This *CSIOF Bulletin* presents the final two feature articles which consider Jewish and Hindu contexts alongside discussion of Islam. Martin Pakula provides an overview of the complex and intractable Israel-Palestine conflict, while Ian Schoonwater presents a fascinating discussion of Hindu and Muslim approaches to the end of life.

The feature articles are supplemented by two very interesting Communiqués, several reports on recent conferences and a selection of book reviews.

As always, this issue of the *CSIOF Bulletin* does not present monolithic viewpoints, but rather seeks to address areas of community and scholarly debate. We hope that you find this issue insightful, relevant and informative.

Features

9/11 – Ten years on – What have we learned?[1]

Bernie Power

I was living in an unstable Middle Eastern country when the events of September 11, 2001 took place. The views of our Arab neighbours varied greatly. They ranged from exhilaration, to sorrow, from threat to fear, from disbelief to denial. Early TV footage showed a large Arab woman dancing with joy on the streets of Jerusalem as the Twin Towers fell. Some of my neighbours believed the tragedy was Allah's judgement on America for its pride, greed, immorality and support for Israel. Others expressed their regret and told me sorrowfully: "This is not how Muslims should act." But as Westerners went about in the Arab streets, occasionally a local person would make a throat-slitting gesture with an index finger. Such people considered Osama bin Laden a hero (although he did not claim responsibility for the attacks until 2004) and he became widely known in the Muslim world as "The Sheikh". Others denied that any Muslims were involved at all, claiming it was a Jewish conspiracy to discredit the Arabs, or a CIA plot to regain funding following the end of the Cold War . As the stock markets plummeted, it was uncertain that the West could recover. "Amereeka finished!" a long-bearded Yemeni tribesman told me, dusting his hands together in contempt.

The US response was measured and calculated. Within a few days, President George Bush stood in a mosque in Washington, declaring that "Islam is a religion of peace." This at least helped to quell the attacks on foreigners within the US, where strong anti-Islamic feeling arose. A few months later, however, US and other coalition troops were in Afghanistan, to kill or capture those they deemed responsible for this atrocity, including Osama bin Laden. Ten years on, the troops are still there. Although bin Laden is now dead, the

---

[1] This article first appeared in the October 2011 edition of *Equip*, EA Ethos' magazine.

Taliban continue to fight on, with the support of large sections of the population of neighbouring Pakistan and other countries.

In 2003, with the mistaken belief that Iraq possessed weapons of mass destruction, the US, UK, Poland and Australia sent in troops to oust the dictator Saddam Hussein. One hope was to plant a stable model democracy in the Middle East. Saddam was ousted but the democracy is not yet forthcoming.

Both Afghanistan and Iraq suffered from widespread corruption, state-sanctioned violence and ethnically or tribally-divided populations. It seems that they did not have a monopoly on these things. High population growth, unemployment, lack of investment and poor future prospects eventually became too much for many Arabs in other nations. They decided that radical change was needed. The 'Arab Spring' of early 2011 brought hundreds of thousands onto the streets, protesting against their governments. So far three Arab dictators have fallen and at least two others are in the gunsights of their people.

It was this widespread sense of disjunction and unease which probably inspired the 9/11 attacks in the first place. Muslims are taught in the Qur'an that "you are the best of peoples evolved for mankind." (Q.3:110 – Yusuf Ali translation). As Muslims pondered on their past history of quick conquest, wide colonisation and impressive civilisation, they wondered why they were now in such a weak position. One answer was that they had wandered too far from their Islamic roots. To recapture their former glory some felt that they needed to return to the two activities which had made them great: *da'wa* (proclamation of Islam) to the world and *jihad* against the infidels. Bassam Tibi, Professor of International Relations at Gottingen University, described this attitude in 1996:

> "At its core Islam is a religious mission to all humanity. Muslims are religiously obliged to disseminate the Islamic faith throughout the world: 'we have sent you forth to all mankind' (Saba 34:28). If non-Muslims submit to conversion or subjugation, this call (dawa) can be pursued peacefully. If they do not, Muslims are obliged to wage war against them. In Islam, peace requires that non-Muslims submit to the call of Islam, either by converting or by accepting the status of a religious minority (dhimmi) and paying the imposed tax, jizya. World

peace, the final stage of the dawa, is reached only with the conversion or submission of all mankind to Islam."[2]

Inspired by teachings from the Qur'an and the Hadith (traditions) which tell of Muhammad's involvement in 28 military excursions, jihadists have launched over 17,000 fatal attacks throughout the world since 9/11, with suicide bombs as their weapon of choice. High-profile targets have included Bali (twice), London, Madrid and Bombay, but most attacks are on a smaller-scale and are unreported in the media. Jihadist efforts have resulted in over 90,000 deaths since 9/11. Many planned attacks have been foiled. In Australia, all 20 of those currently in prison and all 38 of those awaiting trial under anti-terrorism laws are Muslim. So too are the 18 banned organisations listed by ASIO. The recent attack in Norway notwithstanding, Islam seems to have all but cornered the terrorist market.

Any criticism or questioning of Islam over the past ten years has often fetched a sharp rejoinder. The 'Muhammad cartoons' of 2005/2006 brought violent protests around the world resulting in over 100 deaths. In September 2006 Pope Benedict XVI addressed a meeting at Regensburg mentioning Islam's violent history. As a result there were demonstrations in many places with churches burnt and Christians killed.

Other Muslims have chosen a more peaceful path. One month after the Pope's speech, 38 Islamic scholars, representing all branches of Islam, signed "An Open Letter to the Pope." One year later, 138 Islamic representatives co-signed an open letter entitled "A Common Word between Us and You." This was authored by Prince Ghazi bin Muhammad of Jordan. The title of the letter is based on a verse in the Qur'an (Q.3:64) which calls Christians to embrace Islam. However this letter emphasised the common call to love God and love your neighbour. It was not without theological controversy, claiming that "Muslims recognise Jesus Christ as the Messiah, not in the same way Christians do (but Christians themselves anyway have never all agreed with each other on Jesus Christ's nature)." It admitted that "Islam and Christianity are obviously different religions." Despite this, the initial response from many Christians has been positive. One month later a letter by

---

[2] Bassam Tibi "War and Peace in Islam", in Terry Nardin, ed., *The Ethics of War and Peace: Religious and Secular Perspectives* (Princeton University Press 1996), 130.

Christians sought rapprochement with Islam and asked for forgiveness from the Muslim community. Signatories included many evangelical leaders such as John Stott, Bill Hybels and Rick Warren. The Common Word movement has since spawned many international conferences and connections between Muslims and Christians are expanding.

These two approaches – jihad and dialogue – are parts of the spectrum of Islamic reactions since 9/11. Other Muslims are convinced neither of the necessity of violence nor the need for discourse. Among those who go to the West, there are divisions. Many want to assimilate as much as possible into the new country. 70% of the world's refugees are Muslim. They are tired of the wars, oppression, corruption and poverty which characterise the places they have left. They want to enjoy the benefits of stable and just societies, with free speech and a fair reward for their effort. They crave a better future for their children and they want to contribute to their new home. Among these, many have abandoned or reduced their commitment to Islam. "Only about 30% of Australian Muslims are religiously observant," states Melbourne commentator Waleed Aly. (Interestingly I found a similar abandonment of Islam amongst university intellectuals during a recent visit to Iraq.) Those who come to the West wanting to assimilate are the 'immigrants'.

Others come as 'colonists'. They yearn to establish the utopian Islamic state which has eluded them in their own countries. Many wish to remain apart from Westerners and to live under Sharia law. This separation strategy has been championed by the Muslim Brotherhood. Its chief jurisprudent, Sheikh Yusuf Qaradawi, urges Muslims to relocate to Europe, Australia, and North America. There, he says, they should live among other Muslims, conduct their affairs in accordance with Sharia, and pressure Western governments to accept the primacy of Sharia in Muslim enclaves — enclaves that will grow and spread and connect. By convincing "Western leaders and decision-makers of our right to live according to our faith — ideologically, legislatively, and ethically," Qaradawi reasons that Muslims would "traverse an immense barrier in our quest for an Islamic state."[3] The Australia Federation of Islamic Councils (AFIC), the peak Muslim body, has recently called for a 'legal pluralism', allowing some aspects of Shari'a law to be practised by Australian Muslims.

---

[3] http://www.familysecuritymatters.org/publications/id.10264/pub_detail.asp

Although this particular initiative was quickly rebuffed by the Attorney-General, Muslim calls for cultural and religious accommodation have found fertile soil. In a desire to avert further terrorist attacks, Western governments have actively courted Muslim leaders, making many concessions to their demands. The hope is to bring Muslims more into the mainstream. At the same time, the lure of Arab oil money and its investment potential has caused Western governments, including Australia, to move towards Sharia compliant financial policies.[4] Criticism of Islam has been discouraged, and the term 'Muslim terrorism' was dropped from government documents. Islamic organisations were generously funded in the hope that they would undertake activities which would result in greater integration of Muslims. The message of Islam was openly promoted through Australia's 'Living in Harmony' program, where Muslim spokespersons received hundreds of thousands of dollars to endorse a peaceful version of Islam in schools, government offices and official contexts. The Howard Liberal government established a 'Muslim Reference Council' to advise it on policy matters, and the Gillard Labor government recently-announced a ten member Multicultural Council which has five Muslims, but no Chinese, Indian or Aboriginal representatives.

At the same time, some Muslims have implemented a reverse assimilation policy seeking to attract Westerners into Islam. Islamic organisations have ramped up *da'wa* efforts. Tens of thousands of converts to Islam have been reported in the US with claims that the rate of conversion has quadrupled since 9/11. Some commentators cite the Stockholm syndrome, where victims begin to sympathise with and identify with their violent captors.

Rather than hanging their heads in shame or apologising for the 9/11 atrocities carried out in their name, some Muslims have turned it to their advantage. Claiming that they have been stereotyped, a victim mentality has been nurtured among Muslims and some are quick to take legal action when they feel their rights have been infringed. Those who dare to question or criticise Islam are called racist or islamophobes, effectively closing down debate about the nature of Islam.

---

[4] See discussion of Islamic finance later in this Bulletin.

So the picture that emerges is a complex one. The Islamic community, whether worldwide or in any particular country is not united. Muslims adopt a range of positions particularly vis-à-vis the West. The diagram below shows some of these:

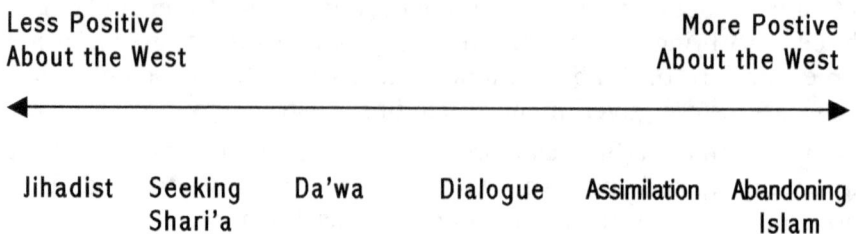

Those seeking to engage with Islam will need to identify what type of Muslim/s they are dealing with.

One might wonder if there is any good news out of all of this. From a Christian perspective, the answer would be "sometimes, yes." It is true that the situation for persecuted Christians in Muslim countries has become worse. The church in Iraq has been decimated by an orchestrated campaign of bombings, killings and kidnappings, and many Christians from the traditional denominations have fled. Yet many Iraqi Muslims, disgusted with Sunni killing Shia and vice versa, have turned to Christ. This is part of a world-wide trend. The events of 9/11 revealed a face of Islam which many Muslims now despise, and they have begun to look in other places for a source of spiritual nourishment. Many have experienced hospitality in the Christian community. As they come to the West fleeing war and poverty, they are often met by Christians who operate out of churches or in Christian organisations providing emergency accommodation, food banks, English lessons and practical help. Some Christians have travelled down the dialogue path, seeking to discover common links between Islam and Christianity. Other Christians have employed 'resistance thinking' to speak up about Islam and expose its violent texts, history and current practices. They have engaged Muslims in debate on issues of theology and public policy. Both approaches have led to an increase among Christians of knowledge about Islam. Others have taken advantage of the influx of Muslims into the West, as skilled migrants, students or refugees, to engage them evangelistically, with positive results. With Islam in the forefront of people's minds, the number of missionaries to Muslims, of those willing to travel to Muslim countries for the sake of the gospel, has mushroomed since 9/11.

The outcome has been a significant increase in the number of Muslims coming to Christ, perhaps at a greater rate than at any other time in history.

In seeking to understand the deeper meaning of 9/11 and how we should respond to Muslims, one can only think of the statement of Joseph to his brothers, his former tormentors: "You intended to harm me, but God intended it for good to accomplish what is now being done, the saving of many lives." (Gen.50:20 NIV) For this we must praise God.

Engaging with a Multifaith Society: why bother?[5]

Peter Riddell

Australians completed a national census on 9 August, for what was the nation's 16th five-yearly count. Much interest surrounds the outcome of the question relating to religious affiliation. Australian censuses have long included such a question, in the process gathering a rich supply of information on the religious profile of the Australian community.

The Growth of the Multifaith Society

The last century of censuses provides evidence of the country's changing religious make-up, as seen in Figure 1.[6]

Figure 1

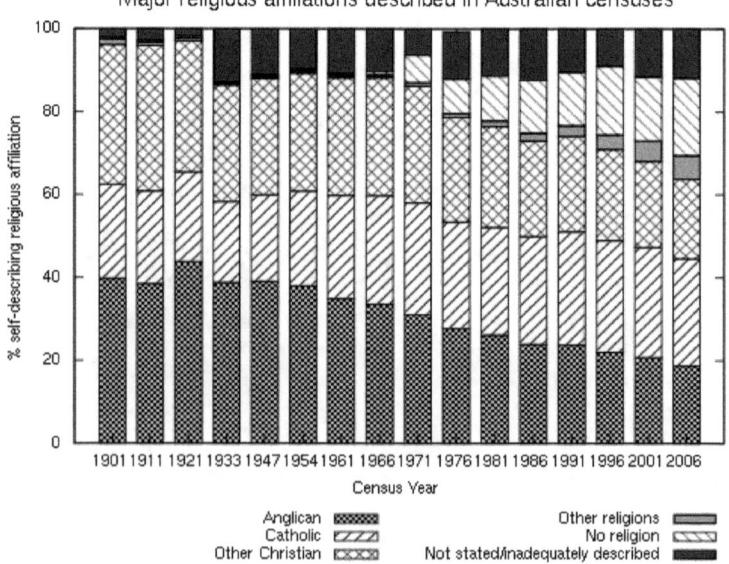

---

[5] This paper was delivered at St Mark's Anglican Church, Forest Hill, Melbourne, on 12 June 2011.

[6] http://upload.wikimedia.org/wikipedia/en/thumb/2/28/AustralianReligiousAffiliation.svg/500px-AustralianReligiousAffiliation.svg.png (11 June 2011).

A steady decline in the proportion of Christians in Australia can be seen during the 20th century. In more recent years, while the numbers of people self-identifying as Christians has remained steady at around 12.5 million since 1991, the numbers of adherents of non-Christian faiths have steadily increased. The last census in 2006 recorded the presence of some 418,000 Buddhists and 340,000 Muslims in Australia, along with lesser numbers of Hindus, Jews and other faiths. If we focus on national statistics, the demographic changes seem relatively gradual. However, if we focus on some city suburbs, such as Sydney's Bankstown, the changes are much more striking over the last 20 years, with Anglican numbers decreasing by 15%, Uniting Church by a similar percentage and Presbyterians by 12%, whereas Buddhist numbers increased by almost 49% and Muslims by 38% in the same period.[7]

In reflecting on these changes, we will focus upon three principles: first, People versus Theological Systems; second, what I call the Multi- Trap; third, approaching other religious systems.

Principle 1: People versus Theological Systems

As we consider how to respond as Christians to our increasingly multifaith society, a first key principle needs to be identified; namely, the importance of a dual method of approach. One angle of approach considers the people of other religions as people, not as representatives of a faith system. The opposite angle of approach considers the other religions as theological systems. It's important not to mix up the two.

Growth in other faith numbers

The growth of the Muslim community in Australia has attracted much discussion. Muslims more than trebled in numbers between 1986 and 2006. Of the 340000 Muslims in Australia in 2006, some 100000 lived in Melbourne. The census figure for Muslims is expected to rise considerably in the 2011 count, because of larger refugee numbers from Iraq, Afghanistan and Somalia, as well as increasing family reunions.

---

[7] http://ultibase.rmit.edu.au/Articles/online/reid1.htm#Appendix2 (11 June 2011).

Figure 2

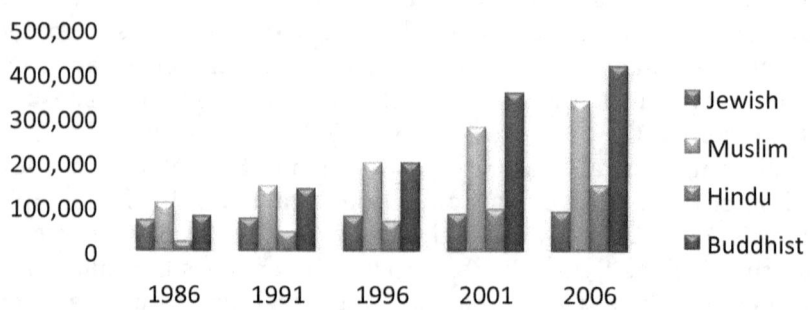

Interestingly, the growth in Buddhism in Australia has been even greater than the increase in Muslim numbers. Buddhists have increased more than fourfold in number between 1986 and 2006 to reach 418,000. This is due in large part to immigration from Buddhist nations such as Vietnam, China and Thailand, though also relevant are the significant numbers of conversions to Buddhism from the majority Anglo-Celtic community.

Though numbers of Hindus are considerably fewer than Buddhists and Muslims, their rate of growth outstrips either of the other two, increasing sevenfold between 1986 and 2006, to reach a community of over 148000 in the latter year, with some large, flourishing Hindu temples in Australian cities.

According to our first Principle, it is key to see the people – Muslims, Hindus, Buddhists – as human beings with daily concerns, needs, hopes, aspirations just like ourselves; namely raising the family; educating the children; finding work; paying the bills. It's in seeing people of other faiths in all their humanity that we can make connections and build bridges.

The Bible provides the model here. Jesus never hesitated to see people as people, rather than reacting to them according to some stereotypical view of following a different faith. For example, he didn't hesitate to speak with the Samaritan woman in John 4 even though "his disciples ... were astonished that he was speaking with a woman) (John 4:27). In Matthew 8:5-13, Jesus didn't hesitate to show compassion to the Roman Centurion who begged him to heal his servant, even though the Centurion was not Jewish and represented the hated Roman occupiers; i.e. Jesus was able to see the person beyond the stereotype. Likewise Ruth was welcomed when she returned from Moab with Naomi to Naomi's people in

Bethlehem, in spite of her different faith and cultural identity. One of the most touching moments in the Bible is the compassion shown by Boaz to Ruth in response to her foreignness and her poverty (Ruth 2).

Principle 2: Beware the Multi- Trap

However, in approaching other faith adherents, we need to be aware of a particular trap that I call the Multi- trap. We often encounter this in interacting as Christians with broader, secular society.

Our diverse society now includes many different languages, races, cultures and faiths. We have been conditioned for a generation not to judge negatively these differences. So **multi-lingual** is good, because no language is better than another; they are just different; e.g. English, Russian and Chinese etc. Similarly **multi-racial** is good, because no race is better than another; they are just different; e.g. Caucasian, Asian, African etc. Furthermore **multi-cultural** is good, because no culture is better than another; they are just different; e.g. Indonesian, Eskimo, Aboriginal.

And therefore, ever so subtly, we have been conditioned that another multi- is simply about difference: **multi-faith**. This produces the idea that multi-faith is good, because no faith is better than another; they are just different; e.g. Christian, Muslim, Hindu, Buddhist etc.

But for me this is a bridge too far; an assumption that should not be accepted without question. How could we accept that all religions are equally valid variations on a Godly theme without taking a good look at them, by studying them. For example, some ancient cults sacrificed babies to stone gods. Should we accept uncritically that such a religion is equally valid as any other? If we don't accept this, then does that mean that perhaps there is a hierarchy of religions, with different levels of truth claims across the faiths?

My conclusion is that there are clearly degrees of truth across the faiths. This is not simply a matter of rational thinking; it is in keeping with Biblical examples. So while Jesus and Paul engaged compassionately with people of other faiths, that did not mean that they accepted uncritically the faith systems that those people embraced. On the contrary, the Bible – both OT and NT – is full of clear statements rejecting aspects of other faiths. In other words, the Bible is not a multi-faith manual.

Consider Jesus' statements to the Samaritan woman at the well (John 4:3-42):

> John 4:22: You worship what you do not know; we worship what we know, for salvation is from the Jews. 4:23 But the hour is coming, and is now here, when the true worshipers will worship the Father in spirit and truth, for the Father seeks such as these to worship him. 4:24 God is spirit, and those who worship him must worship in spirit and truth."

Consider also Paul with the Athenians (Acts 17:16-34)

> Acts 17:22,23: Then Paul stood in the midst of the Areopagus and said, "Men of Athens, I perceive in all things you are very religious; for as I was passing through and considering the objects of your worship, I even found an altar with this inscription: TO THE UNKNOWN GOD. Therefore, the One whom you worship without knowing, Him I proclaim to you."

Furthermore Ruth's statement to Naomi bears close thought:

> (Ruth 1:16–17) Ruth says, "Entreat me not to leave you, or to turn back from following you; For wherever you go, I will go; And wherever you lodge, I will lodge; Your people shall be my people, and your God, my God. Where you die, I will die, and there will I be buried. The LORD do so to me, and more also, if anything but death parts you and me."

So we are called to grapple with the difficult issue of relative truth claims across the faiths, which brings us to our third and final principle.

Principle 3: Considering other religious systems

The third principle is the opposite side of the coin to the first principle; namely, the need to separate religious systems from the people who follow those religions, and the need to consider and evaluate those religious systems in developing Christian responses.

Of the other religions, the ones we have most mentioned are Hinduism, Buddhism and Islam. It is important to note areas where our own Christian faith is in agreement with these other faiths.

Like Christianity, Hinduism believes that death does not mean the end of everything, but a person lives on in some form. Like Christianity, Buddhism shows great compassion for human suffering, with the Buddha's teachings about suffering and compassion being as central to Buddhism as are these concepts to Jesus' Sermon on the Mount. Like Christianity, Islam believes in a

Creator God, prophets, angels and a Day of Judgement, and attributes importance to Jesus as both a prophet and a Latter Day figure. Such points of agreement can provide fruitful materials for interfaith dialogue, and such dialogue activities have become commonplace in recent decades.

But that's the easy part. What about those areas of significant difference between Christianity and these other faiths? For example, Hinduism believes in multiple gods, and prioritises duty to one's foreordained path based on caste above discarding that caste duty for ethical reasons. As for Buddhism, Classical Buddhism simply rejects the concept of God outright. And mainstream Islamic teaching holds that Jesus was not crucified, the Bible has been corrupted, Paul hijacked Jesus' message so the writings of Paul should be ignored, and that Muhammad is the last and greatest prophet, superseding all who went before.

Such differences cannot be reconciled across the faiths. We cannot argue at the same time that there are many gods, there is no god, and there is one monotheistic god: somebody must be wrong. We cannot argue at the same time that Jesus was not crucified and that Jesus was crucified; either Islam or Christianity is wrong on this (and many other conflicting) scores.

So each one of us as Christians has to make a decision where we believe the greater measure of truth lies. After 30 years study of other faiths, I am firmly convinced that the Bible and Christianity provide the greater measure of truth and insight into God and the story that surrounds him.

In considering other religious systems, we must make some judgements and decisions about those systems. Where we believe them to be wrong, we need to find ways of saying so, by seeking to share the truth of Christianity with people of those other faiths.

Engaging with the Multifaith society: Preliminary thoughts on methodology

Our main task in this paper has been to focus on the why: why bother engaging with people of other faiths. What about the how? How should we do so? We will offer here some preliminary thoughts.

Let us first consider some developments on the political stage. New South Wales Member of Parliament and head of the Christian Democratic Party, Fred Nile, has called for a 10 year moratorium on Muslim immigration.[8] While the CDP is a very small party, some members of the state and federal parliaments from mainstream parties have expressed increasing disquiet at the growth in Muslim numbers. But these concerns have attracted strong criticism from members of the political centre-left, who argue that the Muslim community in Australia is quite diverse. This debate is likely to increase in intensity and volume in coming years as the Muslim community continues to grow.

Interestingly, the growth in Buddhism has not attracted the same sense of disquiet among mainstream Australia as is the case with the growth of Muslim numbers. Buddhists have tended to be far less politicised and also far more inclined to integrate with the majority community over time through intermarriage and cultural and religious adaptation.

This issue illustrates the difficulty of striking the right balance between Principles 1 and 3. On the one hand, we should compassionately and hospitably engage with the people of other faiths – in this case Islam – while on the other we should be ready to critique the faith systems that they represent. Rev. Nile's approach risks conflating the two, with the result that legitimate questions about the faith system of Islam risk causing a backlash against people who subscribe to the Islamic faith.

The highly controversial Muslim billboards campaign in Sydney illustrates this dilemma: how should we respond? Principle 3 calls on us to challenge the content of the billboards: is the Jesus of Islam the same as Our Saviour whom we call on in Christianity, and if not, what are the key differences? Some Sydney Christians have responded very skilfully along these lines: see articles in *Eternity* magazine.[9] But Principle 1 calls on us to remain warm and hospitable to Muslims throughout this controversy, not letting it produce anti-Muslim abuse or hostility.

Conclusion

Undoubtedly the growth in other faiths in Australia presents both a challenge and an opportunity to the Australian churches. Many are taking up the challenge, with a visible increase in evangelistic efforts

---

[8] http://www.cdp.org.au/federal-policies/islam.html (19 September 2011).
[9] http://eternity.biz/news/why_the_muslim_billboards_are_good_for_jesus/;
http://eternity.biz/news/responding_to_a_public_slap/1106101444/ (11 June 2011).

among other religious communities on the part of some of the churches. Australia is approaching a watershed moment in terms of its religious identity, and Australian Christians need to marshal their forces in order to face up to the challenges.

A Reflective History of CRIB (1998 –)[10]

Bryan Knell[11]

The story of CRIB starts in 1991, when the European Evangelical Alliances called a conference in the Netherlands, at the De Bron conference centre, called Eurom 91. This conference brought together between 200 and 300 Christians from all across Western Europe who were involved in ministry to Muslims. I estimate that between 25 and 30 of them were from the UK.

At the conference the delegates from each country met separately to consider Muslim outreach in their own situation and following the conference they were encouraged to maintain their national groupings. Colin Chapman became the person who convened the UK group and a small number met a couple of times a year following the conference. The group was called 'The De Bron Group'.

In November 1997 a conference called 'Faith and Power' was held in London. As a result of this event, two 'organisations' came into being although neither of them had any official legal status.

Faith and Society

'Faith and Power' soon changed its name to 'Faith and Society'. This group was designed to bring together evangelical Christians and Muslims. Previously there had been meetings between Christian and Muslims, but the Christians were so theologically mixed that the evangelicals often felt they had so little in common with the other Christians that it was extremely difficult to talk to Muslims in a united way. Many welcomed the opportunity for evangelicals to meet with Muslims. 'Faith and Society' was led by a committee of three Christians and three Muslims and lasted for a few years but then collapsed mainly because it was difficult to get Muslims to attend, even when meetings were held in a mosque.

---

[10] This paper was delivered at a seminar at Melbourne School of Theology on 4 February 2011.

[11] Bryan Knell is a church consultant for Global Connections UK and has led CRIB since its foundation in 1998.

CRIB, Identity and Security

Many Christians in the UK wanted an opportunity to meet to pray for Muslim friends and discuss active evangelism amongst Muslims in Britain. CRIB was launched at a conference held at Hothorpe Hall in Leicestershire between the 11th and 13th March 1998 and entitled 'Faith, Power and Weakness' – a conference on Christian Responses to Islam in Britain. In contrast to 'Faith and Society', CRIB started as a rather secretive group. Many of those involved had been in the Muslim World or wanted to return there and did not want to be linked to or associated with anything that had a public face. Some only used their first name or a pseudonym when they came to CRIB events. There were also some BMBs in CRIB who had major personal security concerns. CRIB has always respected these concerns. Today, we recognise that CRIB is known in the public arena and we are not secretive about its existence, but the dates and venues of its events are not publicised.

From the very beginning, CRIB has had a brief mission statement. We have tried to keep it central to all we do and refer to it constantly.

CRIB's Mission Statement

CRIB is a network for Christians who are involved in evangelistic engagement with Muslims and Islam in Britain with the following goals.

To provide an opportunity for regular meeting, networking and sharing of ideas and resources.

To foster mutual respect and unity among Christians.

To develop credible strategies for the church in responding to Islam in this country.

CRIB National Conference

The main event in the CRIB calendar is the national conference every other year. Conferences held so far are as follows:

1999: *Evaluating Resources for Ministry*

2001: *Swords into Ploughshares: Building relationships with Muslims*

2003: *Swords into Ploughshares: Trinity and Islamic diversity*

2005: *The Muslim friendly church*

2007: *Equipping the church: How to Reach and Nurture Muslims*

2009: *Between Hostility and Naivety: Christian Approaches to Islam in Britain Today*

These conferences have been hugely successful. Almost 200 people were involved in the 2009 event.

CRIB Regional Events

From the beginning there have been CRIB day conferences at various places around the UK, including Birmingham, Derby, Chesterfield and Cambridge.

In about 2000, a regular London CRIB was established which has met at the beginning of March and October each year since.

In 2010, a CRIB North was launched with day conferences in Bradford and Manchester. This is likely to continue for those in the North of the UK.

A CRIB Book

Following the 2009 conference, which many thought was one of the best, it was decided to try and get many who had contributed to the conference, and some others, to contribute to a book with the same title. *Between Hostility and Naivety: Christian Approaches to Islam in Britain Today*, edited by Steve Bell and Colin Chapman has now been written and is due for publication in September 2011.

CRIB Unity

People who work with Muslims are usually very forceful characters with strong personalities, so CRIB has not been without its tensions. We have tried from the beginning to hold together a wide spectrum of evangelicals and generally, with a few exceptions, we have managed to build respect amongst those who disagree. There are those in CRIB who support a polemical and confrontational approach with Muslims and try to challenge fundamental Islamic dogmas and those who see dialogue as the right approach. Some are supporters of 'The Insider Movement' approach and others have serious problems with it.

CRIB is a fellowship of those who have a passionate love for Muslims and believe that they need to come into a relationship with God through Jesus Christ. Consequently, those who promote a hatred of Muslims or hold a strong right wing political position are unlikely to be part of CRIB. At the other extreme, those who think there is salvation through the following of orthodox Islam would not be comfortable in CRIB.

'Grace' Approaches

Towards the end of 2007, three UK Christians who were very involved in Muslim ministry happened to meet together at a conference and started talking about the need to think and plan about the training of Islam amongst Christians in the UK. This was provoked because a couple of key teaching posts in Islamics had recently become vacant and it looked that at least one of them would not be replaced. These three decided that they ought to get a group together to discuss this. I was asked to organise it, simply because the three were too busy and as the leader of CRIB I probably knew all the people who ought to be involved. Twenty-three people met at All Nations Christians College for four hours in July 2008. Most were involved in CRIB although not all and their link with CRIB was not a precondition.

We made some plans for training, but as we met it became obvious that one of our main concerns was the fear of Islam that was so prevalent in many UK churches which snuffed out any inclination to reach out to Muslims. This concerned was fuelled by the recently published *Grace for Muslims* written by Steve Bell. A document grew out of our concerns which took the title 'Gracious Responses to Muslims in Britain Today'.

However, at the end of the 24 hours, someone asked the question 'Who are we?' There was no obvious answer to this question because there was nothing that held us together. Since most of the group were members of CRIB, it was decided to see if CRIB would 'own' this document. This proved not to be the case and although most people in CRIB would support the document, it has no status as far as CRIB is concerned. 'Gracious Responses to Muslims in Britain Today' has never been published and is available for those who were at the meeting in July 2008 to use if they think it would be helpful.

Little did we know that at the same time and completely independently an international group was producing a document based on the same concerns. That document includes an 'affirmation' (very similar in length and content to the Gracious Responses document) and a much longer 'exposition'. These documents, which are known as the Grace and Truth statement can be viewed and downloaded at www.grace-truth.info.

CRIB Relational Links

CRIB is not a charity and has no legal or organisational status. Early on, those on the committee believed they needed to be accountable and so CRIB joined the Evangelical Alliance of the UK. In 2009, the CRIB conference decided that it would be beneficial to join up with Global Connections. CRIB is now officially a forum of Global Connections.

British Evangelical responses to Islam: Some key findings

Richard McCallum [12]

For my PhD research, I interviewed 18 of the two dozen or so Evangelicals who are writing and speaking about Islam in the British context and who believe that the Muslim presence is posing urgent questions to the church, which must be equipped to respond to the challenge. I also collected magazine and newspaper articles, trawled the internet and listened to almost 50 conference talks.

Philosopher Jürgen Habermas describes the groups of bourgeois merchants who met in the C18th coffee shops of London to discuss matters of mutual concern as a 'public sphere' which was shaping 'public opinion'. Gerard Hauser and others have built on Habermas' idea and proposed that the public sphere is made up of many 'micro public spheres' linked together as a lattice. I developed this concept and suggested that the above Evangelicals have been drawn together around the issue of Islam in Britain and through their discourse form a 'religious micro public sphere'.[13]

		Response to Muslims	
		Confrontation	Conciliation
Manner of response	Dogmatic	Dogmatic confrontationalist	Dogmatic conciliator
	Pragmatic	Pragmatic confrontationalist	Pragmatic conciliator

---

[12] Richard McCallum is a freelance researcher, trainer and consultant on Christian-Muslim relations who recently completed his PhD at the University of Exeter.

[13] McCallum, Richard (2011) 'Micro Public Spheres and the Sociology of Religion', *Journal for Contemporary Religion*, 26/2: 173-187.

What I found was that **there is an increasing degree of polarization** within this sphere between those Evangelicals who take a *confrontational approach to Islam* and those who adopt a more *conciliatory approach*.[14] The diagram at the end of this article illustrates the polar extremes of these positions.

Some clearly focus more on *the threat that Islam as a religious system poses* to Britain and the church; others focus more on *the need to understand Muslims as people* and offer them 'risky hospitality'.[15]

Those who are theologically 'conservative' and those who see Islam as a monolith tended to be more negative about Muslims. Those who describe themselves as 'open Evangelicals' and those who see Islam as being diverse were more sympathetic.

Those who had spent time living in the Muslim world (especially Arab countries) and those who had ongoing friendships with Muslims tended to be more irenic than those who had not lived in the Muslim world or had no Muslim friends. However, many of the more irenic interviewees regretted that they now have little time to maintain their friendships with Muslims outside of formal meetings.

Controversial topics dealt with – and disagreed upon – by these authors and speakers included:

- What is Islam and who are the 'true Muslims'?
- What was the source of Islam?
- Is Allah the God of the Bible?
- Is Islam inherently violent?
- Is there an Islamic agenda for global political domination?
- The problems of multiculturalism in Britain.
- The perceived 'Islamization' of British public life in the spheres of politics, law, finance and culture.

The *Common Word* initiative (published in October 2007 – the month I started my research) also provided a rich vein of data. Responses accentuated the pre-existing tensions and served to heighten the polarization. In particular it highlighted a sharp controversy over the interpretation of the Islamic doctrine of *taqiyya*

---

[14] Based on types developed in Bennett, Clinton (2008) *Understanding Christian-Muslim Relations: Past and Present* (London: Continuum).
[15] Marty, Martin (2005) *When Faiths Collide* (Oxford: Blackwell).

(dissimulation) and how widespread its practice may be. Some felt the *Common Word* to be one such example; others vehemently protested this.

By and large conciliatory authors tended to draw on the work of a previous generation of *theologians* including Cragg, Newbigin and the reformation theologians. Confrontationalists invariably went straight to the Islamic texts themselves with no reference to Christian theological thought.

There was general agreement that Christians and Muslims should engage in a *robust dialogue* that should include tackling difficult questions and socio-political issues. There was disagreement, however, over whether this debate should be polemical in nature.

Some of these national figures have sporadic access to the national media, particularly the broadsheet newspapers, and others are occasionally consulted by public bodies. However, in general they find it hard to make their voice heard. Some have started their own websites or blogs and ones utilizes YouTube video. Getting a public hearing is a challenge.

It also became clear that this Evangelical public sphere could not be isolated from the wider public sphere and indeed from the 'Muslim public sphere'. Frequently comments made by Evangelicals are picked up by both Muslims and journalists – especially through the medium of the internet. Intra community discussions are no longer private and contributors must reckon that their views will be overheard by the public at large.

Finally, there was evidence of an unfortunate proximity between certain confrontational positions and some more extreme right wing political views extending from the UK Independence Party (UKIP) to the British National Party (BNP) and its proxy the *Christian Council of Britain*. Identities are blurred by the national media and extremists occasionally quote Evangelical authors.

I then interviewed leaders in 14 large churches in London from across the Evangelical spectrum including conservative, open, charismatic, Pentecostal and different ethnic backgrounds. Their combined congregations represent some 7.5% of Evangelicals in Inner London and more than 1.5% of the total in England.

Of the 14 leaders interviewed most were not overly concerned about Islam and did not consider equipping their church members to relate to Muslims to be a high priority. They certainly did not share the urgency exhibited in the national debate.

I was surprised at how little influence the national 'experts' seemed to have in the London churches included in the study. Their books are not widely read by church leaders and most of them have never been invited to speak in London.

Amongst the national 'experts on Islam' only the names of Patrick Sookhdeo, Colin Chapman, Martin Goldsmith, Michael Nazir-Ali, Jay Smith and Amy Orr-Ewing were known to more than 50% of the church leaders. Only five of the national 'experts' had ever been invited to speak at one of the churches and leaders rarely recommended books on Islam to their congregation with the most popular being Chapman's *Cross & Crescent*, which had been recommended by 5 of them.

Three of the churches run an occasional seminar or training course on Islam and three others include it as an element of existing training courses. None of the churches utilize existing course material such as the *Cross & Crescent Study Guide* (CMS) or *Reflecting on Islam* (Faith to Faith).

Some sociologists assume that the only way a religious community can remain strong is to retreat from society and engagement with other 'out-groups'. Others see the only option as a religious 'crusade' against other points of view. Christian Smith, however, an American sociologist, believes that Evangelicals can remain strong when they adopt an 'engaged orthodoxy', that is when they confidently interact with other groups in society and yet do not compromise their core beliefs. The challenge for the Evangelical church in Britain is to boldly engage with Muslims without retreating quietly on the one hand or confronting aggressively on the other.

In this spirit a 'third way' dialogue which focuses not so much on theology as on 'Muslims and Christians living in society' has been proposed by *Barnabas Fund*.[16] I recently took part in such an event, the *Building Hope Conference,* organized by the *Reconciliation Program* at Yale, at which 'progressive conservative', 'mid-career' Christian, Jewish and Muslim academics and leaders met together and

---

[16] http://www.barnabasfund.org/Barnabas-Fund-Response-to-the-Yale-Center-for-Faith-and-Culture-Statement.html (see particularly the conclusion).

discussed tough issues such as religiously motivated violence, apostasy, religious freedom, Israel-Palestine and evangelism.[17] This experience again confirmed to me that a **robust but fair engagement** holds out the best hope for both social harmony and the advance of God's kingdom in Britain.

My full thesis can be read at http://hdl.handle.net/10036/3129

---

[17] See my report 'A Rabbi, A Priest, and An Imam...' at www.yale.edu/faith/rp/rp_hope.htm#mccallum.

The spectra of Evangelical responses to Islam

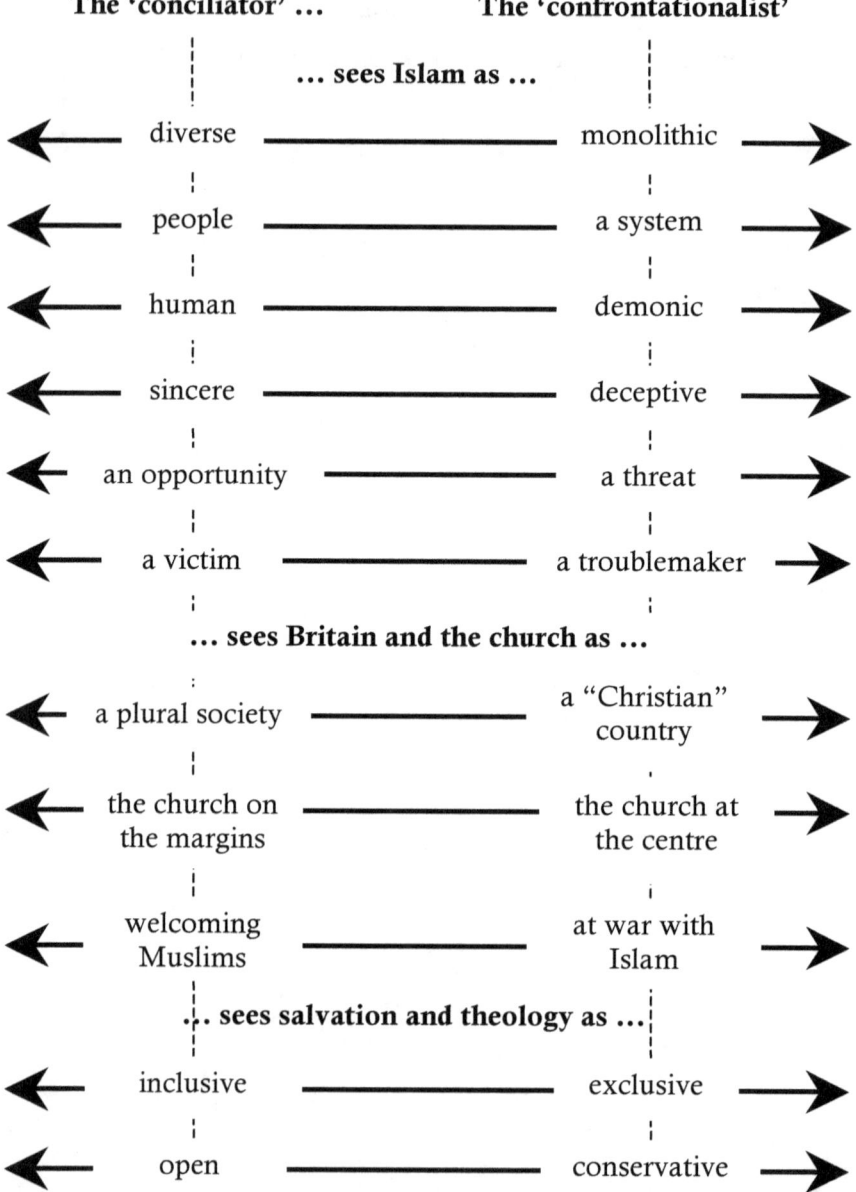

It should be noted that these views represent the extreme poles of thinking on the different issues. Few Evangelicals position themselves at the extremes of all these spectra. Most take up a variety of intermediate positions depending how dogmatic or pragmatic they tend to be.

Dialogue on Social Concerns in Britain: Faith and Society (1997-2003)[18]

Peter Riddell

Evangelical Christian contact with Muslim communities has witnessed an increasing variety of approaches, including dialogue. One of the most significant initiatives in this regard was the Faith and Society dialogue group in Britain, that ran from 1997-2003.

The Faith and Society group derived from an increasing perception among evangelical groups that there were many areas of shared social concern among Muslims and Christians, and that the potential for partnership on these issues was not being addressed through existing methods of Christian-Muslim interaction. Accordingly, a pilot conference was held at the London Institute for Contemporary Christianity in November 1997, called "Faith and Power". The stated aim of the conference was "to reflect on areas of public life in which Christians and Muslims seek to work out the social and political implications of their faith in an increasingly secular society in Britain today."

This conference included plenary presentations on issues of social concern by Christian and Muslim speakers, including Bishop Lesslie Newbigin of the Church of England, Professor Lamin Sanneh of Yale Divinity School and Professor Tariq Modood of the University of Bristol. The plenary presentations were followed by meetings of focus groups addressing specific themes. The Christian: Muslim ratio at this initial conference was 9:1, of an overall attendance approaching 200 people.

In the wake of the inaugural "Faith and Power" conference, a meeting of the organising committee was held on 6 January 1998. Members deemed the "Faith and Power" conference a success, but it was felt that there should be a better numerical balance between the faiths in future gatherings. Subsequent committee meetings in March and April 1998 led to the formal establishment of an ongoing

---

[18] This paper was delivered at a seminar at Melbourne School of Theology on 4 February 2011.

dialogue group, under the leadership of Canon Christopher Lamb, Interfaith Secretary of the Church of England.[19]

A second conference for the renamed Faith and Society group was held on 7 October 1998 at the Islamic Foundation in Leicestershire. The theme was "People of Faith in Britain Today and Tomorrow", with the Christian plenary speaker being Canon Christopher Lamb and Dr Ataullah Siddiqui of the Islamic Foundation in Leicester. It was attended by around 140 people, with the Christian: Muslim ratio being approximately 60:40.[20] Of this number, around thirty-five expressed interest in participating in regular meetings of focus groups.[21] As a result, focus groups on Family, Sexuality and Gender, Education, and Religion and Public Life were convened in February and March 1999 to discuss relevant issues of common concern to Christians and Muslims.[22]

In October 1999 the Faith and Society group held its third annual meeting in Birmingham, and attracted around 100 Christians and Muslims, of whom around 80% were Christian.[23] The theme was "Seeking the Common Good". Reverend John Austin, Bishop of Ascot, Birmingham delivered a plenary presentation on behalf of Christian participants. He called on the audience to learn to tell their respective stories in "an inclusive way". He further lamented the state of economic imbalance in the world and called on people of faith to overcome jointly "the idolatry of economic concerns" in the modern world. Unlike Bishop Austin's presentation, which was virtually devoid of references to biblical text or overtly Christian discourse, Imam Abduljalil Sajid, a leading figure in the Muslim Council of Britain, set his plenary presentation firmly within an Islamic theological framework. Imam Abduljalil argued that the notion of the Common Good was heavily embedded within the vocabulary of the Qur'an, and the five pillars of Islamic duty were

---

[19] Around the same time, a separate group focusing on mission and evangelism, called *Christian Responses to Islam* (CRIB), was established under the chairmanship of Bryan Knell, Head of Arab World Ministries UK. *Faith and Society* and *CRIB* were not organically linked but had some common membership.

[20] The 1997 and 1998 conferences are discussed more fully in Ida Glaser. "Faith and Society in the UK." *Transformation* 17.1 (January/March 2000): 26-29.

[21] *The Faith to Faith Newsletter* No. 1, November 1998, 1.

[22] *The Faith to Faith Newsletter* No. 2, April 1999, 4.

[23] Peter Riddell "Christians and Muslims are 'seeking the common good'", *The Christian Herald*, 23 October 1999, 3.

an effective device for encouraging Muslims to build concern for others into their daily lives. Imam Abduljalil called on people of faith to work together to increase the public role of religion.

Both keynote speakers agreed that dialogue did not demand complete compromise, and that different faiths involved in interfaith co-operation should take care to preserve their distinctive features and beliefs. There was also agreement on the need to address the world-wide imbalance in the distribution of resources and wealth.

During the afternoon, participants broke into five focus groups, addressing a range of social issues: the media; family, sexuality and gender; religion and public life; education; and law. The media group based its discussion around the question of "How to get God in the headlines". Members agreed to seek to identify people of faith in the media who could increase the public profile of religion. Members also agreed to lodge complaints when material offensive to religious concerns appeared in the media.

The group discussing family, sexuality and gender considered a practical case study of family breakdown, and underlined the importance of support and education in the early stages of family formation. In a similar vein, the religion and public life group considered several practical case studies, showing co-operation between Christians and Muslims in various British cities. The education group initiated plans for visits to mutual places of worship by Christians and Muslims. The Law group addressed the different philosophical bases to English and Islamic Law, and considered the challenge ahead with the advent of European laws in Britain.

The annual day conference for the Faith and Society group for the following year was held on 28 October 2000 in Bradford at the Carlisle Business Centre. The theme was "Faiths in Society: A Challenge to Policy Makers", and the particular focus fell on Bradford, which contains a significant Muslim population. The event attracted around 90 participants, of whom approximately one quarter were Muslim.

The day began with reflections on Christian and Muslim scriptures. This was followed by a Christian plenary session, given by Guy Wilkinson, Archdeacon of Bradford. He spoke of the church's perception of its own place and of that of the Muslim community, and then considered the public policy perception of religions. He concluded by suggesting ways that Christians and Muslims could jointly engage with public society, calling for joint action on social issues, co-operation to address negative media images of religious communities, and efforts to overcome territorial separation (stating that "white flight" is the church's responsibility and that Muslims should not encourage territorial separation).

The Muslim plenary address was given by Mohammed Ajeeb, former Lord Mayor of Bradford. He called for frankness and honesty in dialogue, and cited instances of how Muslims had been victims of Islamophobia in Bradford and elsewhere in Britain. He stressed that Muslims perceived the Church as influential in public society, and called on the Church to assist the Muslim community in its situation of relative disempowerment.

In small group discussion, responses were given to the plenary talks. Some participants commented that significant public resources were channelled into the Muslim community and other minority communities in Bradford. One Asian Christian present asked how Muslims in Bradford contributed to the common good, rather than merely focusing on Muslim rights. This led to considerable discussion between Muslim and Christian speakers present. Focus groups met in the afternoon, assembled according to the topics of Law, Media, Education, Religion and Public Life, and Family, Sexuality and Gender

In the crisis surrounding the 9/11 terrorist attacks, the Faith and Society event planned for late 2001 did not proceed. After a two-year hiatus, a group of Christians and Muslims[24] met on 29 October 2002 to plan a resurrection of the dialogue group. This meeting set the topic for the next conference in 2003 as "Faith and Citizenship". Committee members agreed to seek funding from both Muslim and Christian sources, and mapped out the program for the 2003 conference.

The Faith and Society Day Conference of 26 May 2003 was held at the Islamic Cultural Centre, London Central Mosque, in Regents Park. There were 45 attendees, of whom only seven were Muslims, all speakers or committee members.[25] In his welcoming comments,

---

[24] Those present were Canon Michael Ipgrave (Chair), John Webber, Julian Bond, Peter Riddell, Saeed Abdulrahim, and Imam Abduljalil Sajid.

[25] The poor Muslim attendance was due in part to an almost total absence of advertising of the event among the Muslim community.

Canon Michael Ipgrave set the scene by posing a key question: "We are citizens of this country. We are also people of faith ... How do we belong together and interact with one another?"

The Muslim plenary speaker was lawyer Ahmad Thompson, a white convert to Islam. He began by pronouncing the Islamic profession of faith, the *Shahada*, also quoting from Qur'an chapter 97. He declared that there were two kinds of people in creation: those with faith (*mu'minun*) and those who reject faith (*kuffar*). This division, he explained, would determine their fate: the Garden or Hell Fire respectively. Thompson devoted most of his talk to an expose of the Five Pillars of Islam.

In question time Thompson engaged in extended polemic on political issues, lambasting what he termed "*kafir* [infidel] kingdoms" and tyrannies, including the Pyramid civilization, the Incas, Stalinist Russia, and extending to the USA, commenting "Once America has control of the oil in Iraq, it will be able to eliminate its own balance of payments", and declaring that the Zionists want an empire from the Nile to the Euphrates. His talk concluded with the declaration that "if we people of *iman* [faith] make a stand when people of ignorance control society, we can transform society."

The Christian plenary speaker was Dr Derek Tidball, Principal of the London School of Theology.[26] He argued that "the Christian life cannot avoid addressing engagement with the world. But we cannot read straight off the page from Scripture." He pointed out that the Bible does not portray Christians living in a democracy. Therefore, he added, "we need hermeneutics to relate Scripture to the modern world." Tidball drew on four "moments in Scripture" (Israel as theocracy, the period of exile, the period of Jesus Christ, the period of the Apostles), then addressed the challenge of relating Scriptural principles to the modern world, concluding that "to require religious people not to participate in politics is in effect to disenfranchise a section of the population."

In further discussion, Ahmed Thompson called for every religious community in Britain to be self-governing, and that ecclesiastical councils, the Jewish Beth Din and Sharia Courts should all be recognised by the legal authorities of the land. In response, one

---

[26] Dr Tidball's presentation is published in this issue of the CSIOF Bulletin.

Muslim participant said: "Thompson speaks as if there is nothing positive about the West. That worries me." Thompson commented further: "It is important to understand why there are laws. For example, don't shun pork simply because it is prohibited. We should understand that the meat is bad. It is the only meat that goes bad from the inside out."

The 2003 Faith and Society conference proved to be the final event of this group. Throughout its life it had been beset by several main problems. The first was the ever decreasing Muslim attendance, culminating in the 2003 meeting where virtually no Muslims from the general community participated. Furthermore, some unreasoned polemic from certain Muslim speakers, combined with some bland, self-effacing presentations from certain Christian speakers, created more dissonance than consonance among the audience, discouraging the kind of commitment needed for such dialogue groups to survive and flourish.

Nevertheless, Faith and Society provided an example of how evangelical Christian approaches to other faiths have diversified beyond traditional mission activities. In the early years (1998-2000) Faith and Society facilitated significant and ongoing contacts between evangelical Christians and Muslims in Britain. Though its discussions ostensibly addressed issues of social concern, nevertheless scriptural and theological references were also frequent from both sides, and provided an opportunity for Christians and Muslims to engage as people of faith, as well as common inhabitants of British society.

Faith-Full Citizens:

Christians and Muslims in Britain[27]

Derek J. Tidball[28]

Seventy-five years ago my grandfather, a small town businessman and elder in a Pentecostal Church, was contemplating entering local politics. One day he visited the council offices as he was prayerfully musing on the question in his mind. There he encountered a door with a 'No entry' sign displayed on it. He took that as a sign from God and decided there and then never to have anything more to do with politics, though it never stopped him from having strong opinions which he dumped on the family! With great respect I believe him to be wrong.

Christian discipleship has been all too often interpreted as having to do with the next life and nothing to do with this life. But the God of the Bible is a God who created human beings to live in relationship with one another and who pronounces solitude and isolation – cut-offness — to be 'not good'. He creates not only the physical world as the sphere in which men and women are to live but the social world, creating institutions through which we can relate with one another, institutions like that of the family, tribe, law, economy and government.[29] He consistently works within human culture, most notably in the incarnation of Jesus Christ, and demonstrates, once the original human creation had been damaged through sin, a passion to recreate a humanity that would reflect his character of holiness, righteousness, justice, mercy and love. The ultimate vision of the Christian faith is of a future, not where men and women live in an ethereal state of disembodied souls, but where the heavens and the earth are recreated, creation itself is restored, and men and

---

[27] This paper was delivered at the Faith & Society Day Conference, held at the Islamic Cultural Centre, London Central Mosque on 26th May 2003.

[28] Derek Tidball was Principal of London School of Theology from 1995-2007 and is currently Visiting Scholar at Spurgeon's College, London.

[29] For an excellent exposition of some of these areas see Christopher J. H. Wright, *Old Testament Ethics for the People of God* (Leicester: IVP, 2004).

women are reconciled to one another, with God himself taking his rightful place in their midst.

The Christian, then, cannot avoid coming to terms with how they are to act out their Christian responsibility in this world and especially in the particular group of people to whom they belong, that is, in the nation of which they are citizens.

Affirming these doctrines as our starting point does not permit us to go on to read straight off the page of scripture how we are to act in the contemporary, pluralistic and democratic societies of today where the mindset, at least in the U.K. (the USA is somewhat different) is almost totally secular in its handling of public affairs. Although they lived in a pluralistic world, the Bible nowhere portrays the disciples of Jesus living in a democracy, nor in a secular culture. The world of the Bible is one which is alive with, albeit diverse, religious worldviews. This does not give us permission to put the Bible on one side as irrelevant since it has much to teach us but it does cause us to handle it with hermeneutical wisdom.

Illustrations from biblical history

Let me illustrate its relevance by briefly sketching four moments in Biblical history:

First, there was the nation of Israel as a theocracy.

The Old Testament refuses to countenance the popular division between sacred and secular and testifies rather to the Lord God as sovereign over the whole of life. Take the Book of Leviticus, often wrongly regarded as the most arcane of OT books, as an example. It begins with detailed regulations about worship, which in fact have much to do with restoring the balance of creation. It continues from as early as chapter 9 onwards, but especially from chapter 17 to the conclusion of the book in chapter 27, to turn to matters of diet, disease, sexuality, wealth, race relations, land economics, the aged, the disabled, the economically marginal. Its agenda reads very much like a contemporary political agenda. God reigned over the whole of life, in the social and economic life of the community as much as the religious life of his people.

Since we no longer live in a theocracy where the nation has entered into a covenant with God, it is not an agenda that can be imposed on people by law; nor should it be. But, Christians, as heirs of the Jewish revelation about God, will realize that two things, at least, will follow. First, they should understand that God is not just God in the sanctuary; he longs to be God in the kitchen, in the bank, in the bedroom, the health clinic, the butchers and the boardroom as well. Secondly, they can digest the wisdom of and reasons for the legislation of Leviticus and see why and how it produced a wholesome, caring and just society. They should then argue the case, suitably translated to the forms of the contemporary world, for our adopting some of the same godly wisdom in our nation.

The second moment is that of the exile.

Living in an alien land those children of Israel, like Daniel, Jeremiah and Nehemiah, who desired to be faithful to God had to learn to live not in the theocracy to which they were accustomed but as a powerless minority where other powers held sway. Those powers were political but were supported, as political power always is, by religious ideology and symbolism, to legitimate them and maintain their authority. Daniel has much to teach us in this respect. He was in no position, initially at least, to make demands or pass laws for others to obey. But nor was he required to keep silent. He could challenge the ruling ideologies of his day and request that he be tested against them, at the cost of his own life if necessary. He and his companions never lost sight of the fact that the God of Israel, considered by most to be the tribal deity of a minor and insignificant people called the Jews, was 'the most high God' whose dominion was eternal and whose kingdom endured from generation to generation, who did what pleased him with the powers of heaven and the people of the earth and who was accountable to none (Dan. 4:34).

It is immediately apparent how such a picture is of relevance to those living under oppressive regimes, like those of the former communist states. On a visit to Romanian during the days of former dictator Ceausescu my wife once asked a Christian leader, one who had suffered much at the hands of the securitaté, what limits there were to the freedom with which they could practice their faith. He replied to our initial surprise, 'Dianne, you can do anything you like for the sake of the kingdom of God,' but then he added, 'providing you are prepared to pay the price'. He had been forged on Daniel's anvil. The stance is perhaps less immediately apparent but, I believe, no less relevant, for those of us living in a democracy driven by a liberal agenda and secular political powers.

The third moment is that of the time of Jesus.

His country was occupied by an alien power. The Babylon of Daniel's day was no more. The occupying power was now that of Rome. There were also a variety of religious leaders whose views covered the spectrum of complete compromise with Rome (like Herod) to complete withdrawal (like the Essenes).

His own teaching recognized the reality of the political powers of Rome. His approach to 'citizenship' in such a situation, if we may anachronistically use that word, was complex and we need to nuance our understanding of it carefully. At one level he complied unprotestingly with the law, as when he paid his taxes (Matt. 17:27; 22:19). At another level, he undermined the current regime both by the barely disguised political statements with which his teaching bristles and by his barely disguised political actions, as when he entered Jerusalem on Palm Sunday as 'the Messiah, the son of David'. In doing this he was placing himself inevitably in direct opposition to and so on a collision course with Caesar and the High Priestly authorities of his day. At yet another level, he is driven by the awareness of an altogether different kingdom, as he told Pilate, Caesar's powerful representative in Judah (Jn. 18:36; 19:11). It was the will of the sovereign in this kingdom that would prevail and therefore Jesus submits himself to death, believing that through it forgiveness of sin and new life would come.

At various times we are called to be fully and compliantly involved in our nation and at others to undermine its conventions and power structures just as Jesus did, since we too owe allegiance not ultimately to a nation but to one living God. As a recent illustration of just such a stance we should thank God for the confessing church in Germany who stood against Hitler in the last war.

The fourth moment is the time of the apostles and the mission of the early church.

Their social context was much more akin to our own context today. Christians were a tiny minority living without power or influence in a pluralistic world. There was no reason why anyone should take notice of them and they would struggle to make their voice heard, especially in 'the corridors of power'. Yet they did so. They did so surprisingly not by addressing issues of social, economic and political concern directly, as we can see from their apparent acquiescence in slavery as an institution. They did so by proclaiming the sovereignty, Lordship and Messiahship of Jesus, the unique Son of God. Typical of this is the claim made in Colossians 1:15f. that declares Jesus to be pre-eminent in the totality of his creation, whether past, present or future. Jesus, not Caesar, was Lord. This belief is captured in Abraham Kuyper's comment that, 'There is not one part of creation over which Christ does not proclaim 'It's mine'''.

This message proved of strategic relevance to their mission because first, this single claim led to an ethical stance that undermined the political and social conventions of the ancient world, as Rome was to discover before many years had passed. We need to bear this in mind and hold it in tension with other teaching of the apostles that seems negligently complacent about injustice. In Romans 13, for example, we read of the importance of the role of the government. Christians are instructed to pay their taxes so that the government might achieve its purposes (13:7). 1 Timothy 2:2-3 urges prayer for rulers, so that harmonious and peaceful communities might be experienced. 1 Peter 2:13-17 calls for Christians to submit to authorities and honour the king and does so against a backdrop of unjust suffering. Human authority is recognized as a God-given means of creating and maintaining just and wholesome societies. But human political authority is always subordinate to Christ's divine authority and, when it fails by stepping beyond its power, or fails to fulfill its responsibilities it is subject to God's judgment (see Revelation 13).

Working out these principles in a democratic society, rather than an imperialistic one, implies the need to play one's full part as citizens, using the opportunity of debate afforded by freedom of speech, of expressing one's views, rather than remaining silent and of active participation in voting and in other ways, rather than of non-involvement. It calls also for more than talk but for the involvement of Christians in voluntary service with a view to the practical building of a healthy society.

Contemporary application: But how?

The question arises, however, as to how one is to apply these examples and principles in practice in a pluralistic world. Christians have adopted different answers to this with some taking a priestly standpoint which argues for the need to stand alongside the establishment and act in the role of its chaplain. Others have argued for a prophetic ministry that stands over against the mainstream and distances itself from the establishment. The former leads sociologically to a church-type organization and the latter to a sect-type orientation. But here I want to think more about political and moral arguments than sociological relationships.

The standard approach to the involvement of Christians in the political sphere, as the philosopher Paul Weithman[30] has called it, is to argue that if religious people do want to be involved they must put their religious views to one side and only engage in the political debate by using arguments that are accessible to all. Since religious reasons are not accessible to all, religious people, if they wish to participate must translate their ideas into those which are, that is to a lowest secular or humanitarian common denominator, and thus make their appeal widely. They must do this, or exempt themselves from political engagement, in the interests of civility, trust and mutual respect. Weithman has shown that such an argument is philosophically indefensible and pragmatically misguided. People's religious views provide them with a holistic worldview that leads them to arguments that justify their desire for particular legislation. Providing they hold the views responsibly and are willing to put them in the public arena they should not be prevented from doing so. The argument that such discourse should be excluded from the public arena is actually also based on 'religious' argument and a 'theological' worldview, albeit a different one, from the Christian worldview. It is not a neutral argument.

On the pragmatic question: religion, far from being detrimental to political involvement, has been found by extensive sociological research to play a positive role because (i) churches sensitize people to political issues and expose them to politicians, (ii) it gives people political skills, (iii) it encourages their involvement and (iv) provides them with a coherent framework with which to think issues through. Without religion many would not be involved as active citizens at all. To require religious people not to engage in political activity for religious reasons 'is to require citizens to withdraw from democratic politics' and in effect to disenfranchise a large section of the population. Weithman's arguments and the research he quotes can be supplemented by a mountain of evidence from elsewhere. It has most recently supported by the extensive investigations of Robert Putnam in *American Grace*.[31]

---

[30] See Paul Weithman, *Religion and the Obligations of Citizenship*, Cambridge University Press, 2002.
[31] Putnam, *American Grace: How Religion Divides and Unites Us*, New York: Simon & Schuster, 2010. See especially his chapter called 'Religion and Good Neighbourliness', 443-492.

Let me mention some other relevant factors, almost at random:

(1) Historically, the British Labour Party owes more to Methodism than to Marxism. In my university days in the north east of England, I grew to have enormous respect for the education and skills of the Durham miners whose informal education had taken place in the village chapels. On this, the 300 the anniversary of Wesley's birth,[32] the contribution of Methodism in particular and of nonconformity in general, to the shaping of the United Kingdom, through active political involvement, should be acknowledged.

(2) Churchgoers are three times more likely to be involved in assisting in some voluntary association than non-churchgoers.[33] The church employs twice as many youth workers as local authorities do. These channels form the web that holds society together. If the government want active citizens who will create and maintain healthy community relationships they should be aware of the need to work with, not against, the churches and to do so in such a way that enables churches to maintain the integrity of their particular faith position rather than being forced into some vague compromised form of generic faith commitment. Thankfully, the Chancellor of the Exchequer, at least, has shown some recognition of that in supporting, for example, ventures like Faithworks.

(3) There is a widespread belief that evangelicals, especially of a more fundamentalist kind, are seeking to create a nightmarish, reactionary society, which is discriminatory in the areas of race, sex and sexual preference, as well as reactionary in its view of criminal punishment and opposed to freedoms recently gained in relation to life-style choices. Again, serious research shows that such a view needs demythologizing.[34] In spite of all the rhetoric employed by its more fundamentalist spokespersons evangelical Christians are

---

Putnam shows, for example, that active church goers have a much higher rate of volunteering and not just in religious organizations, and are more generous in making philanthropic donations, again not just to religious causes, than those who are not active in church. He writes, 'In round numbers, regular churchgoers are more than twice as likely to volunteer to help the needy, compared to demographically matched Americans who rarely, if ever, attend church' (p. 446). Research in the UK presents a similar picture, See *21st Century Evangelicalism*, London: Evangelical Alliance, 2011.

[32] This refers to the date on which the original paper was given.

[33] On this whole area see Robin Gill, *Churchgoers and Christian Ethics* (Cambridge: Cambridge University Press, 1999), *passim*.

[34] See Christian Smith, *Christian America? What Evangelicals Really Want* (University of California Press, 2000). See also Putnam, *American Grace*, e.g. 308-319.

quite able to state their case reasonably and negotiate their way around the realities of living in a pluralistic world comfortably, without personally giving up on their convictions.

(4) Our political leaders need to consider seriously the argument that a world based on secular principles, devoid of religious motivation, justification, symbolism and ritual is unlikely to generate enough energy to convince people to behave in the required socially constructive ways. It does not sufficiently inspire the 'spiritual' imagination that people need to relate in a socially cohesive way. We have moved from arguing that the dignity of each individual is based on the fact that they are made in the image of God to a vacuous attempt to legislate about human rights based on some vague humanism. The British Chief Rabbi, Lord Sacks, says, 'The Enlightenment gave us the concept of universal rights, but this remains a thin morality, stronger in abstract ideas than in its grip on the moral imagination.'[35]

(5) There is mounting evidence that the customary evangelical strategy that we change the world by changing or converting individuals one at a time so that they adopt a Christian worldview is inadequate, if not misguided, as a strategy for transforming society. It fails to appreciate the deeper sociological and political dimensions which are involved in the way in which a nation or society operates. Deeper and more complex strategies are necessary if society is to be transformed for the better.[36]

Conclusion

Notwithstanding Weithman's powerful argument, it may be that like Hezekiah, when threatened by Sennacherib's invading army, as recorded in 2 Kings 18-19, we have to speak two languages – the language of faith behind the wall of the religious community, and the language of international diplomacy on the wall of public affairs. 'People of faith', says Walter Brueggemann, must be bilingual'.[37] We must certainly concede that when the public language is being spoken believers have no special privilege or advantage. But we must constantly remind ourselves that conversation 'on the wall' is crucial, as well as conversation 'behind

---

[35] Jonathan Sacks, *The Dignity of Difference* (Continuum, 2002), 112.
[36] See James D. Hunter, *To Change the World, The Irony, Tragedy and Possibility of Christianity in the Late Modern World* (Oxford: Oxford University Press), 2010.
[37] Walter Brueggemann, *Interpretation and Obedience* (Fortress Press, 1991), 41-69.

the wall'. The people who attack the practitioners of faith won't go away, any more than Sennacherib's army would disappear from the walls of ancient Jerusalem; at least not without divine intervention. But unless the conversation behind the wall is actively maintained, believers will capitulate to unbelief and other perceptions of reality will take over. Conversations behind the wall are crucial: they have a prior claim; they do not accommodate or compromise. But those who have such conversations should try to translate their beliefs, in so far as possible, into another language, although it may not always be possible to do so. We believe we owe it to the nation to continue to speak of spiritual issues and values, to argue for particular interpretations of the world and to pursue particular ethics and moral positions. We also believe we owe it to the nation to be actively involved in binding people and communities together through service, creating a more healthy society than the one we currently experience. That is what it means to be 'faithful' citizens.

Strangers in the Land[38]

Moyra Dale[39]

Muslims are increasing in both numbers and visibility in Australia today. This paper discusses some of the different sources of our information about them, and how they contribute in understanding both the numbers and nature of these communities. Then we ask what the Bible suggests about attitudes to minorities: and finally consider our response to their presence as our neighbours.

Understanding

Media

The first source of our information is usually the media. Here we have to read critically, knowing that media presentation is guided by what is most newsworthy rather than trustworthy, as well as by political guidelines of sponsors and readership. Acts of terrorism, discussion of high visibility markers such as the burka, controversies around building new mosques, are good news value and given a prominent place in news reports. Controversy attracts listeners to talk-back shows. How are we to find a Christian perspective between the extremes of demonizing all Muslims, or an unthinking adherence to political correctness?

For example, the media attention focus on Islam leads many to think that it is the fastest growing minority religious group in Australia. However a closer look reveals that Buddhism is growing much faster, and may be doing much more to erode basic Judeo-Christian values. We share with Islam a belief in one God, His sovereignty, and that that has implications for every part of our lives. Buddhism refuses even the existence of a personal God. And its denial of the validity of suffering and personal responsibility for

---

[38] This paper was first delivered on November 6, 2010 at the CSIOF Spring Symposium that addressed the theme "The Numbers Game: Australia's Changing Demographic and its Implications for Christian-Muslim Relations". A report on this Symposium appears later in this issue of the CSIOF Bulletin.

[39] Moyra Dale teaches in the area of intercultural and interreligious studies, as an adjunct lecturer at Ridley College and visiting lecturer at other institutions.

other's suffering undercuts some of the historical events and values most foundational to Australian society, such as Gallipoli, and the significance of those who have (and still are) prepared to lay down their lives to safeguard freedom.

Statistics

Another source of information is statistics. Demographic statistics give us more concrete information about numbers of Muslims, including countries of origin, birth rates (and how these change over generations), localities of residence and population concentration, occupation and education. We can differentiate between permanent migrants, refugees, and those who have come for a few years as students. We can measure rates of immigration against rates of emigration back to the source country. We see where Muslims are among measures of disadvantage, such as unemployment and lower income levels. And so we begin to gain a more accurate understanding of Muslim communities here.

Surveys give us some understanding of attitudes, and so of the extent of more radicalized forms of Islam. While the shape and context of questions can influence answers, and they are not infallibly accurate predictors (witness the recent Victorian state elections!), they are nevertheless a useful indicator of shifts in attitudes and values. Riaz Hassan's book *Inside Muslim Minds* is an invaluable discussion of attitudes across the Muslim world.

Putting flesh on the bones of statistics

Numbers give us a broad overview of what is happening. However we need to flesh them out, to understand how and why shifts in population or opinion are taking place. Rigorous ethnographic studies are important here: but they can be harder to access from academic journals or conference papers.

More immediate and widely available are books written by those we might call 'distant insiders' – people who are within the Muslim community but have been able to step back and write from a more distanced perspective. Just a few of the many examples include Hanifa Deen's *Caravanserai*, on the Muslim community in Australia and particularly in Lakemba. *The Islamist* by Ed Hussein is an invaluable description of the dynamics of extremist Muslim groups attracting youth in the U.K. Ayaan Hirsi Ali's *Infidel* gives insight into patterns of authority, decision-making and control within

Somali communities worldwide. These books contribute a richer understanding of how different Muslim communities function, with competing tensions and shifts of power within them.

On the celluloid front, films like *Yasmin* (in the UK Pakistani community) and *Veiled Ambition* (Lebanese Muslims in Australia) illustrate the tensions of 2nd generation British or Australian Muslim young women.

Personal acquaintance

Sources published, printed and filmed help us know about the Muslim communities, but we can't neglect the fourth dimension – that of personal acquaintance. As Christians, we are very aware of the difference of knowing about Jesus, and knowing Him in personal relationship. So our understanding of Islam and Muslims should always be informed by personal relationships with Muslim friends.[40]

There are plenty of examples to show that robust ideological engagement doesn't preclude genuine friendship, even with the most radical adherents of Islam. Rather it enhances and gives integrity to the debate. Of the many Muslims in Australia, very few have been welcomed into a Christian home. Ed Hussein's book is notable for his lack of Christian friends. It begs the question whether, if every Christian in Australia had a Muslim friend, we would face far less issues with Islamic extremism.

A Biblical Perspective

Statistical, sociological and personal knowledge inform us. But as Christians we cannot let them alone guide our response, but must rather ground our reading in a Biblical understanding. How does the Bible shape our thinking about migrant communities, and those who are ethnically and religiously different to us?

Settle in the land

What can we learn from the Israelites' sojourns as minorities in another country? We look back to the small community of the sons of Jacob that moved to Egypt and stayed there for 400 years until

---

[40] As helpfully explored in Tony Payne's book, *Islam In Our Backyard*.

they became a 'great nation' in the land (Gen 15:13; Exodus 1:5-7): and to the group of Israelites taken into Babylonia in exile for seventy years (Jer 29:4-14). These movements were constrained by famine and war, not unlike the reasons that bring many Muslims into western countries. When we examine Israel's experience as a minority community, three points stand out.

i). They were *not* to integrate with the surrounding nation. The small group of Israelites retained their pastoral pursuits in Goshen, separate from the agriculturally-based Egyptian society around them. The exiles in Babylon were not to bow down to Babylonian idols, nor even to compromise their laws of food and ritual purity (chapters 1 and 3 of Daniel).

ii). They *were* to settle down and to work and pray for the welfare of the country where they were living (Jer 29:7). God blessed not only the Israelites, but preserved the economy and population of Egypt through Joseph's leadership during the years of famine. Daniel (and his friends) had leading roles as advisors during the reign of successive kings in Babylon. Nehemiah and Mordecai also had trusted positions in administration in the non-Jewish states where they worked.

iii). Their experience of exile, of minority community life, deeply shaped their own self-awareness and identity, and also the attitudes and behaviour that God called them to demonstrate to aliens living among them (Dt 10:12-22: 24:19-22).

The example of Israel in a minority context can help us in thinking about the place of minority groups among us. Moucarry argues that migrants today "should play their full part in the life of the larger community, for their own sake as well as for the sake of their home country."[41] But we need to go further in considering how God's people were to relate to minorities and those of different ethnic-religious backgrounds among them.

Aliens in the land

Out of their own experience in exile, the Deuteronomic code called the Israelites to care for the strangers who lived among them, for the sake of God who "executes justice for the orphan and the widow,

---

[41] Moucarry, 287.

and who loves the strangers, providing them food and clothing." God's imperatives include both practical help and also attitudes. They were told to "love the stranger, for you also were strangers in the land of Egypt," (Dt 10:12-22).[42] Memory of the stay in Egypt was to help them ensure that they did "not deprive a resident alien or an orphan of justice," and that they left harvest gleanings for "the alien, the orphan and the widow," (Dt 24:17-22).[43] "The legal provisions often grouped together the strangers, the Levites, the poor, the widows and the orphans so as to emphasize the precariousness of their lives".[44] The insistence on worshipping God alone was coupled with the duty of care for the 'resident alien' (Ex 22:20,21). The command to love one's neighbour was placed alongside the command to "love the alien among you as yourself" (Lev 19:18, 34).

Their role as God's special people did not mean that the Israelites could have a privileged position over strangers living in the land: rather they were to live out their covenant relationship with God by caring for the rights and needs of resident aliens, according them the same legal rights.[45] God's people were to be characterized by their wholehearted love for God alone,[46] and also by their care for strangers among them.[47]

"But I say to you ..."

The New Testament is not silent about how we relate to those beyond the fold of faith. Jesus was characterized by association and eating with those who were outside the righteous religious. He outraged his hearers by pointing to God's grace among non-Jews

---

[42] And Ps 146:9.
[43] Also Lev 19:10, 23:22.
[44] Moucarry, 285.
[45] See Moucarry, 285, for the references giving more detail about specific legal provisions for strangers in the land.
[46] Dt 6:5; 7:9,12; 10:12; 11:1, 13; 13:3; 30:6.
[47] Generally intermarriage with non-Israelites was frowned on because they might cause their spouses to worship other gods (Jos 23:12; 1 Ki 11:2;, Ezra 9). However the book of Ruth stands in opposition to this, where the non-Israelite spouse is drawn to worship the One God, receives the care that belongs to strangers and widows, enters the family of the kinsman-redeemer and so becomes part of the lineage of the true Redeemer. So at least three of the women in Matthew's genealogy (Tamar, Rahab and Ruth) were foreign wives. Bathsheba was married to a Hittite, although she may herself have been from Judah.

(Lk 4:21-30). He performed miracles of healing at the request of non-Jews, and commended them for their faith (Mt 8:5-13, 15:21-28, Lk 17:11-19). Then (as now) patriotism was one of the most highly commended values. In that context, Jesus put care for the enemy above nationalism, eating with those who collaborated with the occupying army (Lk 19:1-10), telling his own followers to go beyond compulsion in helping the occupying forces (Mt 5:41). And he outrageously took a Samaritan, bitter adversary of the Jews, as exemplar in redefining the 'other' who is our neighbour, and the sacrificial care we are called to in loving the other as myself (Lk 10:25-37).

Jesus reinforces the Deuteronomic commands of total, uncompromising love for God and love for neighbour. In his own example and teaching he goes beyond the command to care for aliens among us, to extend both the definition of neighbour and the practical demonstration of costly love (Mt 5:43-48).

Our response

The people of God

Citizens of heaven

How may we respond as God's people to the Muslim communities among us? Our first response is as God's people before patriots, as citizens of heaven rather than of this land (Jn 18:36; Heb 11:13-16). Early Christians were seen as suspect or subversive because of their refusal to defer to local gods or the emperor cult. Da Silva notes that, "The rejection of the gods by the Christians made them "atheists" and colored them as a subversive element in the society, a potential cancer in the body politic."[48] Christians have always followed Christ's example of the Good Samaritan in going beyond self-preservation or even community loyalty, to care for all those disadvantaged or wounded, regardless of national, ethnic or religious allegiance.

The Bible calls us to costly care, sacrificial love for the strangers among us, a love expressed in hospitality and advocacy.

Care for and table fellowship with all

---

[48] Da Silva, 46-47.

Caring for people in need may be staying with the young bride as she gives birth to her first child in a country far away from her own family, knowing little of the language and culture here as she learns to be a mother for the first time. It may be accompanying a student through a multitude of offices and bureaucratic conversations as he tries to sort out problems with visas or courses. It may be regularly visiting someone in prison who has stabbed someone in a fight, and being ready to read the Bible with him as he seeks Christ's redemption and direction for a messed-up life. It may equally involve caring for the wife who has sought refuge for herself and her children from an abusive marriage, and has little language and no family support. Or speaking up for the follower of Christ from a Muslim background who may face persecution and torture within his family or community or home country for his decision: and may also find lack of understanding or opposition within Australian officialdom. It will certainly involve the hospitality of our homes and lives, in the radically-inclusive table fellowship of Jesus.

Standing with our brothers and sisters

In working for the good of all, we are especially to care for those of the household of faith, bearing each other's burdens.[49] So we become the family of those who have come new into the household of faith from another religious background, with all the pressures involved. There are also our sisters and brothers who are of Christian background, and have come to live here against a background of generations or centuries of pressure living as *dhimmis* under unfriendly government. A number of them show sacrificial courage in reaching out with the good news of Christ to those who were hostile to them, and we must stand with them to strengthen them in prayer and practical support.

Sharing prayer and life

When God's people disobeyed his command to go out to all the earth and stayed put, he intervened to scatter them.[50] He does not let our disobedience thwart his purpose. As part of our call to go to all nations, God has brought peoples to the church here, many from closed countries. As individuals and Christian communities we can

---

[49] Gal 6:2-10.
[50] Gen 1:28 – 11:8,9: Acts 1:8 – 8:1,4.

choose to pray and to live in areas of high Muslim concentration, sharing our prayers and our lives with our neighbours.

Citizens on this earth

Our primary responsibility is to respond from our place as God's people, citizens of heaven. But we still have a responsibility to seek the welfare of the state and community in which we live, and of all the individuals within it.[51] Moucarry lists "religious freedom, tolerance and the primacy of the individual over the community" as core values of pluralistic European culture, and suggests that "The extent to which Muslims are willing to be part of European society will be seen, for instance, in their readiness to respect the decision of a Muslim woman to marry a non-Muslim, or of a Muslim man or woman to convert to a religion of their choice".[52] This area has been extensively dealt with elsewhere (for example in Claydon's book which opens up many of the issues of public policy with regard to Islam and Muslim communities in the West), so will not be explored further in this paper.

Conclusion

A discussion of demographics and survey materials takes us helpfully beyond general media in informing us about Muslim communities in the west. This paper suggests that these resources are helpful, and should be supplemented by ethnographic material and especially by personal acquaintance. A brief survey of Biblical material relating to minority groups suggests ways forward in attitude and practical engagement with the neighbours God has brought us.

References

Ali, Ayaan Hirsi (2007) *Infidel.* New York: Free Press.

Claydon, David (ed.) (2009) *Islam. Human Rights and Public Policy.* Melbourne: Acorn Press

Deen, Hanifa (1995, 2003) *Caravanserai: Journey Among Australian Muslims.* Freemantle: Freemantle Arts Centre Press.

---

[51] 1 Tim 2:1-4.
[52] Moucarry, 288-9.

De Silva, David A. (2000) *Honor, Patronage, Kinship & Purity. Unlocking New Testament Culture.* Illinois: InterVarsity Press.

Hassan, Riaz (2008) *Inside Muslim Minds.* Melbourne: Melbourne University Press.

Husain, Ed (2007) *The Islamist.* London: Penguin Books

Moucarry, Chawkat (2001) *Faith to Faith.* Nottingham: Intervarsity Press

Payne, Tony (2002) *Islam in our Backyard.* Sydney: Matthias Press

Yusuf, Irfan (2009) *Once Were Radicals.* Sydney: Allan & Unwin.

Legislating Against Creeping Sharia in Britain

John Smith (pseudonym)

There is growing concern that Sharia law is being used in England and Wales as an alternative to the proper legal process, especially in family law or criminal matters. In a free society, individuals must be able to organise their affairs according to their own principles, whether religious or otherwise. However, attempting to operate a parallel legal jurisdiction is another matter altogether.

The problem of 'courts' that are not courts

Pressure on the UK court system has increased the use of alternative methods of resolving disputes, such as arbitration and mediation.

Arbitration is where two or more parties agree an independent person who will decide their dispute. If they wish, they can say in advance that the person's decision will be final and binding, and can be enforced by the UK courts under the Arbitration Act 1996. The Act allows parties to agree how civil disputes should be settled, including choosing to settle disputes according to law different to the law of England and Wales. Family and criminal law matters cannot be arbitrated on.[53]

Mediation involves a neutral party trying to help two or more parties reach common ground, a mutually satisfactory agreement. This agreement can sometimes be put before a court. In mediation, the third party does not decide the matter, but helps the parties decide it between themselves.

The bodies which are commonly referred to as 'Sharia courts' appear to operate in a number of guises. Some fall within the arbitration framework, able to make legally binding decisions in legitimate arbitration proceedings. Other bodies have little or no legal status, but still claim to operate within particular communities as if they had the power to making authoritative and legally binding rulings.

---

[53] Arbitration Act 1996, Section 81(1)(a); Edgar v Edgar [1980] 1 WLR 1410; House of Commons, Hansard, 24 Nov 2008, col. 866 wa

Sharia principles are being applied in at least three forums which are of concern:

Arbitration tribunals applying discriminatory rules

The Arbitration Act 1996 has facilitated the establishment of arbitration tribunals operating according to Sharia law. Such tribunals allow parties to settle certain civil (largely financial) disputes according to Sharia law in such a way that the decision can be enforced in UK courts.

The Muslim Arbitration Tribunal (MAT) is the highest profile of the Sharia forums operating under the Arbitration Act. Established in 2007, the MAT has its headquarters in Nuneaton, with additional tribunals in London, Manchester, Bradford and Birmingham.[54]

Arbitration based on Sharia law should be fairly well regulated, because it takes place under the Arbitration Act. The MAT always has a barrister or solicitor of England and Wales sitting as part of the tribunal, which will also include a "Scholar of Islamic Sacred Law".[55]

However, there is a fear that even when these tribunals are operating legitimately they are imbedding discrimination against women. An MAT in Nuneaton adjudicated on an inheritance dispute between three sisters and two brothers. In accordance with Sharia law principles, the men were given double the inheritance of the women.[56]

Since such decisions are given the force of law, it is a matter of serious concern that such discriminatory principles are being applied. The religious freedom to decide disputes in accordance with religious beliefs is something that must be vigorously protected, but when discriminatory decisions are validated by being given the force of law then the law itself is brought into disrepute.

---

[54] http://www.dailymail.co.uk/news/article-1196165/Britain-85-sharia-courts-The-astonishing-spread-Islamic-justice-closed-doors.html (1 June 2011).
[55] http://www.matribunal.com/procedure_rules.html (1 June 2011).
[56] *Coventry Evening Telegraph* (9 September 2008).

Arbitration tribunals acting outside their remit

Arbitration tribunals should only be deciding civil disputes. However, the desire of some adherents of certain religions to settle their disputes in accordance with the relevant religious law extends much further, and there have been reports of tribunals adjudicating on matters such as criminal and family law which are well outside the arbitration framework.

The MAT admitted overseeing six cases of domestic violence, apparently working 'in tandem' with police investigations. In each case the women who had been abused withdrew their complaints from the police, while the MAT judges suggested that the husbands take anger-management classes and advice from Muslim elders with no further punishment.[57]

Sheikh Faiz-ul-Aqtab Siddiqi, chairman of the governing council of the MAT, said in 2008 that he expected the courts to handle a greater number of "smaller" criminal cases in coming years as more Muslim clients approach them.[58] There are clear suggestions that the MAT, despite recognizing on its website that it does not have jurisdiction to deal with criminal offences, may be exceeding its remit in such cases in the name of "reconciliation"[59] or "regulating community affairs".[60]

Sharia Councils, mosques and community elders

The third category includes all other so-called 'Sharia courts'. One report has estimated that there are "at least" 85 Sharia forums in the UK.[61]

Around a dozen of these other bodies are headed by the Islamic Sharia Council, which has been operating since 1982.[62] The Islamic Sharia Council is a registered charity, with courts or councils based in London, Birmingham, Manchester, Rotherham, Bradford and Leyton. The Islamic Sharia Council's own website claims to have

---

[57] *The Sunday Times*, 14 September 2008; *The Daily Telegraph*, 14 September 2008.
[58] *The Sunday Times*, 14 September 2008.
[59] http://www.matribunal.com/cases_faimly.html (2 June 2011).
[60] *The Sunday Times*, 14 September 2008.
[61] MacEoin, D, *Sharia Law or 'One Law for All'?*, CIVITAS, June 2009, page 69
[62] http://www.dailymail.co.uk/news/article-1197478/Sharia-law-UK--How-Islam-dispensing-justice-side-British-courts.html (2 June 2011).

dealt with thousands of cases, mostly relating to matrimonial disputes.[63] As will be seen, there is evidence that many of these 'matrimonial disputes' relate to those who have had a Muslim marriage but are cohabiting under English law as no lawful marriage has been contracted.

Compulsory mediation – a contradiction in terms

There is a legitimate role for mediation in divorce proceedings. Litigation can be adjourned so that disputes about money, property and children can be resolved with the assistance of a mediator. But mediation has to be voluntary. The role of the mediator is as a facilitator to assist an agreement being reached. The mediator is not a judge or an arbitrator who imposes a decision.

A report by the One Law for All campaign described the rather confusing status of Sharia forums operating in a way which mixes up arbitration and mediation:

> "Although Sharia Councils are said to mediate in family matters, they have a different understanding of the term "mediation" and fail to distinguish between mediation and arbitration. Sharia Councils, for example, will often ask people to sign an agreement to abide by their decisions. Councils often call themselves courts and the presiding imams are called judges. According to the British Sharia Council for example: 'In changing times, [the BSC] fulfils the criteria for consultative processes. In regard to domestic problems it works as a Sharia court.' Their decisions are imposed and seen to be legal judgements."[64]

Most of the remaining Sharia forums are operating out of mosques around the country[65] or through other arrangements, such as meetings of community elders, which are being presented within particular communities as making authoritative and legally binding rulings. British Indian author and journalist Edna Fernandes, after her own investigation, concluded that "scores more imams dispense justice through their own mosques" and that "Sharia is being used informally within the Muslim community to tackle crime such as

---

[63] See http://www.islamic-sharia.org/index.php?option=com_content&task=view&id=12&Itemid=27 and http://www.islamic-sharia.org/about-us/about-us-9.html (2 June 2011).
[64] *Sharia Law in Britain: A Threat to One Law for All and Equal Rights*, One Law for All, June 2010, 11.
[65] MacEoin, D, *Sharia Law or 'One Law for All'?*, CIVITAS, June 2009, 69.

gang fights or stabbings, bypassing police and the British court system".[66]

In 2006, Radio 4 was told that a stabbing case was decided upon by an unofficial Somali 'court' sitting in southeast London. The victim's family told the police it would be settled out of court. A Sharia hearing was allegedly held with elders deciding that the assailants should compensate the victim.[67]

The problem of intimidation

At the heart of both arbitration and mediation is the matter of consent. In arbitration, both parties agree to submit their dispute to a mutually agreeable third party for a decision to be made. In mediation, the two parties are voluntarily using a third party to help them reach an agreement that is acceptable to both sides. Concerns about the validity of consent lie behind many of the problems with Sharia courts.

Fariborz Pooya, Chair of the Council of Ex-Muslims of Britain, has said:

> "Sharia law is not voluntary, but rather compulsory by its very nature. To deceptively talk of the voluntary nature of these courts is a means by which Islamic groups give legal cover and pretence to their discrimination. For the Government to accept this argument is akin to outsourcing the legal system to Islamic groups. This is detrimental to, and a betrayal of, the rights of our most vulnerable citizens to being equal before the law."[68]

Robert Whelan, of the Civitas think-tank, has highlighted the "big question over how far submission to Sharia courts is voluntary among Muslim women". He added: "Women who live in some communities may have no option but to go to the Sharia court."[69]

The very existence and legitimisation of Sharia courts puts pressure on vulnerable women not to assert their civil rights under UK law:

---

[66] http://www.dailymail.co.uk/news/article-1197478/Sharia-law-UK--How-Islam-dispensing-justice-side-British-courts.html

[67] *The Times*, 2 December 2006; *The Daily Telegraph*, 29 November 2006.

[68] *Sharia Law in Britain*, One Law for All, June 2010, 18.

[69] See http://www.dailymail.co.uk/news/article-1080509/Islamic-courts-cleared-deal-family-divorce-disputes-Government-endorses-sharia.html#ixzz1O6ZcHjmn (2 June 2011).

Women are often pressured by their families into going to these courts and may lack knowledge of both the English language and their rights under British law.[70]

Refusal to settle a dispute in a Sharia forum could lead to threats and intimidation, or being ostracised and labelled a disbeliever.[71]

Under most interpretations of Islam a person who leaves the faith is an apostate who can be put to death.[72]

Women who ignore Islamic law and obtain only a civil divorce could be declared apostates.[73]

Going to the police is often considered culturally unacceptable and shameful.[74]

Fatwas have been issued which claim that Sharia law takes priority over secular law and therefore many Muslims may not even want to involve secular authorities.[75]

There is a particular concern around domestic violence. Several women's groups say they are often reluctant to go to the police with women who have run away to escape violence because they cannot trust Asian police officers not to betray the girls to their abusing families. In many cases, women fleeing domestic violence have been deliberately returned to their homes or betrayed to their families by policemen, councillors and others.[76]

What has been reported in the press or in academic studies is likely to be the tip of the iceberg. The very nature of the problem means that it is very difficult to provide evidence of its scale. Many who would be able to testify about their experiences are too afraid to identify themselves. The kind of family or community pressure that has been exerted is seen from persistent reports of intimidation:

A pharmacist's assistant in Tower Hamlets has been threatened for not wearing a hijab even though she is not a Muslim. Muslims in

---

[70] *Sharia Law in Britain*, One Law for All, June 2010, 15.
[71] *Sharia Law in Britain*, One Law for All, June 2010, 16.
[72] MacEoin, D, *Sharia Law or 'One Law for All'?*, CIVITAS, June 2009, 5.
[73] *Islam In Britain*, The Institute for the Study of Islam and Christianity, February 2005
[74] Brandon, J. and Hafez, S., *Crimes of the Community: Honour-based Violence in the UK* (London: Centre for Social Cohesion, 2008), 116-117.
[75] MacEoin, D., *Sharia Law or 'One Law for All'?*, CIVITAS, June 2009, 40.
[76] Brandon and Hafez, *Crimes of the Community*, 115-116.

the community threatened to boycott the shop if the assistant did not dress in longer robes and cover her head because the area is a "Muslim area". After approaching the media she was threatened again, this time with death.[77]

In February a man was convicted of threatening to kill his female cousin, and her father, after she refused to wear the hijab.[78]

Last year, a Muslim Labour councillor in Tower Hamlets called in the police after receiving anonymous death threats because of her "Western" dress.[79]

Tower Hamlets religious studies teacher Gary Smith was attacked by four Muslim men on his way to work. The four men all pleaded guilty for GBH with intent. A device placed in one of the men's cars by a policeman for an unrelated matter recorded Akmol Hussein saying: 'He's mocking Islam and he's putting doubts in people's minds". Adding: "How can somebody take a job to teach Islam when they're not even a Muslim themselves?" Mr Smith suffered bleeding on the brain, a fractured skull and a gash on his face.[80]

International beauty contestant, Shanna Bukhari received death threats and online abuse since she decided she wanted to be the first Muslim to represent Britain in the contest. She has to have an alarm to carry at all times and at one point felt forced to hire a private security firm to protect her.[81]

Gina Khan, a woman's rights activist, had to flee her home town of Birmingham after receiving threats from local Islamists when she publicly denounced their teachings on women. As a result she was forced to halt her campaigning and flee with her children to another part of the UK where she now lives in hiding.[82]

An outreach worker from a women's group in one Northern town said that some Muslim men there had formed a group to attempt to

---

[77] *The Sunday Times*, 17 April 2011. See the Communiqué by Alan Craig elsewhere in this issue of the *CSIOF Bulletin* for more information on this case.

[78] Metropolitan Police Service, Press Release, 23 February 2011

[79] *The Sunday Telegraph*, 14 March 2010.

[80] *Metro*, 27 May 2011.

[81] *The Sunday Times*, 1 May 2011.

[82] Brandon and Hafez, *Crimes of the Community*, 86-88.

intimidate female activists which they felt were undermining the image of Asians by publicising the problem of domestic violence.[83]

Maryam Namazie, a former Muslim who founded the Council of Ex-Muslims in Britain, has received numerous death threats for her actions.[84]

Singer Deepika Thathaal has received sustained abuse and death threats from Muslims for her music videos.[85]

In 2007 a Channel 4 *Dispatches* documentary, 'Unholy War', detailed persecution of those who have left Islam for Christianity.[86]

Harry Potter actress Afshan Azad was assaulted by her brother and threatened by her father – resulting in her fleeing in fear for her life – because she had a non-Muslim boyfriend.[87]

Nissar and Qubra Hussein converted to Christianity from Islam in 1996. Following this, Mr Hussein – a hospital nurse from Bradford – and his family suffered a decade of persecution, including a threat to burn down their house. One night the Hussein family awoke to find that the unoccupied house next door was on fire. The family eventually moved out of their home.[88]

In apparent response to his opposition to the Abbey Mills 'mega mosque', Alan Craig of the Christian Peoples Alliance has been the subject of a YouTube video showing his purported obituary, together with that of his wife and two children.[89]

Nobody should have to live in such fear in the UK. The reality of intimidation is proof of the need for legislation to address the

---

[83] Brandon and Hafez, *Crimes of the Community*, 88.
[84] Murray, D and Verwey, J P, *Victims of Intimidation: Freedom of Speech within Europe's Muslim Communities*, Centre for Social Cohesion, 2008, 49-52.
[85] Murray, D and Verwey, J P, *Victims of Intimidation*, 85-89.
[86] *The Independent*, 25 October 2007.
[87] *The Daily Telegraph*, 22 January 2011; *The Daily Telegraph*, 1 July 2010.
[88] *Christian Today*, 17 September 2007. http://www.christiantoday.com/article/bishop.nazirali.warns.of.attacks.on.muslimchristian.converts/13252.htm (3 June 2011); The Daily Express, 30 April 2008; The Washington Times, 27 November 2008; The Times, 28 April 2008; Bradford Telegraph and Argus, 29 April 2008.
[89] *Times Online*, 6 November 2007, see http://www.timesonline.co.uk/tol/news/uk/article2820684.ece (3 June 2011).

problems for women in Muslim communities who wish to stand against the Sharia system but who face pressure and intimidation which inhibit them from doing so.

David Green of Civitas has said:

"The reality is that for many Muslims, Sharia courts are in practice part of an institutionalised atmosphere of intimidation, backed by the ultimate sanction of a death threat."[90]

The problem of 'marriages' that are not marriages

Most Sharia 'courts', when dealing with divorce, are doing so purely in a religious sense. They cannot claim to be a civil court able to grant civil divorce; they are simply granting a religious divorce in accordance with Sharia law. In many cases this is all that is necessary for a 'divorce' anyway – although a religious wedding ceremony has taken place, the marriage has never been registered and is therefore not valid in the eyes of the civil law.

This exposes a problem: women who are married in Islamic ceremonies but are not officially married under English law can suffer grave disadvantages because they lack legal protection. What is more, particularly where English is not their first language, they can be unaware that their marriage is not officially recognised by English law. Only 208 places of meeting for religious worship in England and Wales have been registered by the Registrar General for the solemnisation of Muslim marriages.[91] So the vast majority of mosques[92] in England and Wales are not registered under the Marriages Act, suggesting that many Muslim wedding ceremonies are not forming legal marriages.[93] Unofficial estimates suggest that only around one third of the Muslim marriage ceremonies performed in Britain are registered under the Marriage Act.[94] Luton police pursued a man for bigamy who had married in Luton, then

---

[90] MacEoin, D, *Sharia Law or 'One Law for All'?*, CIVITAS, June 2009, page 5
[91] House of Lords, Hansard, 24 May 2011, col. 422 wa
[92] The number of mosques is estimated to be as high as 1,600, see, for example, Times Online, 30 January 2009. http://www.timesonline.co.uk/tol/news/uk/article5621482.ece as at 3 June 2011; http://www.muslimsinbritain.org/ (3 June 2011).
[93] *The Times*, 29 October 2008 (Letters to the Editor).
[94] *The Bolton News*, 30 May 2008; guardian.co.uk, 8 July 2010, see http://www.guardian.co.uk/commentisfree/belief/2010/jul/08/religion-sharia-marriage-registration-islam (3 June 2011).

flown to Pakistan and married again. The first marriage was invalid as it had been conducted by an imam in an unregistered mosque. His first wife was left with no legal protection by the family courts, and the husband was free to bring his second wife back to Britain as his legal spouse.[95]

The situation was summed up in a 2006 report by Women Living Under Muslim Laws:

> "Many women in Muslim communities in Britain believe (and men who know better can benefit by failing to correct their error) that a marriage in a mosque or before *imams* in Britain constitutes a valid marriage. In the event of a dispute and an attempt to enforce their rights through the British courts, they are shocked to discover that, unless married in one of the very few mosques registered as places for civil ceremony, they are not validly married in the eyes of British law."[96]

Seeking a Solution

The Arbitration and Mediation Services (Equality) Bill brought before the British Parliament on 8 June 2011 is a step in the right direction. It is not the whole solution. It seeks to tackle some of the more flagrant injustices outlined above. It does so, principally, by trying to ensure that Muslim women are protected from discrimination and intimidation, and that any attempts by individuals or organisations to establish a parallel legal jurisdiction in this country are prosecuted as unlawful.

The Arbitration and Mediation (Equality) Bill seeks to:

- Strengthen the duties of public bodies to ensure that women are made aware of their legal rights and to clarify that discrimination law applies to arbitration;
- Strengthen the powers of the police and judiciary to protect women from coercion and intimidation; and
- Prevent the operation of a parallel legal system by outlawing any person, such as a Sharia 'judge', falsely claiming legal jurisdiction in the UK.

---

[95] *The Guardian*, 14 June 2007.
[96] Warraich, SA and Balchin, C, *Recognizing the Un-Recognized: Inter-Country Cases and Muslim Marriages & Divorces in Britain*, WLUML, January 2006, 2.

Islamic Finance: For and Against

Peter Riddell

Islamic financial operations have witnessed a huge and rapid expansion around the world, including the West, in recent years. Described by one commentator as "a cottage industry restricted to a handful of Arab countries only 30 years ago",[97] the Islamic finance industry currently holds assets worth around $1000 billion, registering growth of some 30% in 2009 and 2010, and witnessing the launch of 20 new Islamic banks across the world in 2009.[98]

There are several key factors supporting this growth. First, the huge windfall of revenue due to increase in oil prices from the 1970s onwards provided ample funds for developing this sector. The combined revenue from oil sales of the six member nations of the Arab Gulf Cooperation Council increased tenfold during the first decade of the twenty-first century.[99] The second factor stimulating this boom was the 2008 international financial crisis which threatened a meltdown of the world economy. In this climate, the availability of ready cash in large amounts from Islamic sources has proven to be a lure that many in the West cannot resist.

Furthermore, some Muslims have seen this as providing a historic opportunity to expand the Islamic faith. In the words of prominent Islamist scholar Yusuf al-Qaradawi: "The Western system has collapsed and we [Muslims] have a complete economic philosophy as well as spiritual strength... All riches are ours... the Islamic nation has all or nearly all the oil and we have an economic philosophy that no one else has... [Muslims should] profit from the

---

[97] Kevin Brown, "Wider appeal battles with signs of inefficiency", The Future of Islamic Finance (*Financial Times Special Report*). http://media.ft.com/cms/ac6257de-e2de-11de-b028-00144feab49a.pdf (December 8, 2009).
[98] David Oakley, "Dubai debacle overshadows growth", The Future of Islamic Finance (*Financial Times Special Report*), December 8, 2009, http://media.ft.com/cms/ac6257de-e2de-11de-b028-00144feab49a.pdf
[99] http://www.ansamed.info/en/news/ME02.YAM19005.html

crisis to bring about the triumph of the (Islamic) nation, which holds the spiritual and material resources for victory."[100]

Principles and Methods

The over-riding consideration driving Islamic finance is that financial operations should be consistent with the dictates of Islamic Sharia Law. This legal framework is considered by most Muslim scholars to be from Allah, and therefore not subject to human critique or reproach. Sharia Law encompasses financial matters but goes far beyond them, also covering matters of the family, civil law, codes of punishment which can be quite draconian, and a host of other areas which address the minutiae of people's lives.

Reconciling the dictates of Sharia Law with the detail of international and domestic finances is no easy matter. There are several principles that underpin Islamic finance. First, interest (*riba*) on loans is banned; this inevitably means that Islamic economic operations tend to establish a kind of financial apartheid, given how fundamental the concept of loan interest is to western economics. Second, speculation (*gharar*) is also banned, and transactions must be based on an underlying existing asset or service; "if you are going to trade in an asset you have to own it first".[101]

Third, Islamic finance presents itself as placing special emphasis on seemingly ethical investments. Islamic financial institutions, be they banks, insurance agencies or other Sharia-compliant bodies, avoid all links with institutions dealing in weapons, gambling, pornography, pork or alcohol. Nevertheless, such an approach is equally possible with non-Islamic financial operations and, indeed, there are many Christian financial institutions that prioritize ethical considerations in their operations.

Fourth, Islamic finance commonly operates on a risk-sharing model, whereby a financier will contribute cash and a borrower will contribute expertise in what is portrayed as a partner venture. But David Clark points out the flaw in this seemingly appealing concept: "Upon borrower default the financier will have the right to demand its interest in the *Musharaka* [joint venture] (or the assets

---

[100] "Replace capitalism with Islamic financial system: cleric", *Qatar Morning Post*, 12 October 2008, http://www.qatarmorningpost.com/news/newsfull.php?newid=281538
[101] Saleh Ibrahim, "Islamic regulations can help economies in crisis", *Al Huda* No 34. http://www.alhudacibe.com/AlhudaMagazine/Issue-034/article04.php (May-July 2009).

forming the interest in the *Musharaka*) be purchased by the borrower at the price of the outstanding debt..."[102]

Finally, Islamic finance disapproves of companies that depend too heavily on borrowing, with a threshold seen as 33% of a firm's stockmarket value.[103] Again, this is normal practice for many member organisations of the vast non-Islamic financial sector as well.

In order to ensure that Sharia-based financial organisations are compliant with the above principles, Islamic scholars are engaged by companies to monitor and advise on appropriate policies and procedures. This highly specialised field is being driven by a finite number of scholars who wield enormous power and influence. One particular survey of this scholarly community concluded that "[t]he top six scholars hold 31.7 percent of all surveyed board positions in research by Funds@Work."[104]

Islamic Finance on the March

Although there are presently no global Islamic banks to rival HSBC, Lloyds TSB and such mammoth institutions, this situation is likely to change in the not-too-distant future. Dubai Bank, set up in 2002 before converting to an Islamic bank five years later, set its sights on becoming a major global Islamic lender through acquisitions,[105] though the Dubai economic crisis of 2009 has slowed down such plans.

The rapid emergence of Sharia-banking windows in western financial institutions is noteworthy. The giant HSBC now offers Sharia-compliant services through its Amanah unit.[106] At the end of August 2008 the Swedish Avanza Bank offered its customers a new Islamic investment option, *Selector World Sharia Value*, a global fund of some 110 companies.[107] In Britain, high street banks are also

---

[102] David Clark, "The Islamic Finance myth". http://www.shariahfinancewatch.org/blog/2010/04/23/the-shariah-compliant-finance-myth/
[103] http://www.ansamed.info/en/news/ME02.YAM19005.html (7 October, 2008).
[104] "Factbox: How to take a bank Islamic", Reuters, April 25, 2010.
[105] http://www.forbes.com/afxnewslimited/feeds/afx/2008/08/31/afx5374418.html
[106] http://www.forbes.com/afxnewslimited/feeds/afx/2008/08/31/afx5374418.html
[107] http://www.shariahfinancewatch.org/blog/2008/08/28/swedens-first-sharia-fund-is-being-launched-today/

responding, offering a small range of Sharia-compliant products, including bank accounts,[108] and drawing in Muslim scholars to advise on developing new services. These trends are encouraged by governments; for example, in March 2008 the British Chancellor of the Exchequer announced measures to promote Islamic finance,[109] reflecting the fact that at that time Britain was already the 10th largest holder of Sharia-compliant assets, leading other Western nations.

Furthermore, Britain's first Islamic bank, the Birmingham-headquartered Islamic Bank of Britain, reported significant growth in non-Muslim customers since the onset of turbulence on financial markets in 2008, with Islamic banks claiming to be insulated from the credit crisis,[110] though events in subsequent years cast significant doubts on this claim.

Problems with Islamic Finance

The appeal of Islamic financial institutions and their ways to both Western governments and individuals may well be a poisoned chalice. There are three main areas of difficulty that Western policy makers need consider.

First is the level of debate within the Muslim community worldwide. Sharia finance encounters vigorous opposition from some Muslims due to debate about details of interpretation. In some cases, Islamic scholars understand the term *riba* to mean usury rather than simple interest on a loan. These scholars are more at ease with the concept of interest as understood in the Western capitalist context. On the other hand, those scholars who reject all interest tend to be from the more militant, Islamist end of the Islamic spectrum, the very kinds of Muslims that Western governments should not be encouraging.[111]

---

[108] For example, see http://www.lloydstsb.com/current_accounts/islamic_account.asp (4 October 2008).

[109] *HM Treasury, Budget Report 2008* (London: The Stationary Office, 2008) 46. http://www.hm-treasury.gov.uk/media/9/9/bud08_completereport.pdf (4 October 2008).

[110] http://www.birminghampost.net/birmingham-business/birmingham-business-news/other-uk-business/2008/10/03/non-muslims-turn-to-islamic-bank-as-a-safe-option-65233-21962049/

[111] Patrick Sookhdeo, *Understanding Islamic Finance* (MacLean VA: Isaac Publishing, 2008), 17ff.

Further on the question of debate among Muslim scholars, even those who are closely involved with the sector can at times disagree about the forms that Sharia financing should take. An example of this was the ruling by the International Islamic Fiqh Academy in April 2009 that criticised the widely used *Tawarruq* instrument, suggesting that it too closely resembled conventional loans.[112] This debate highlighted the fact that the instruments of Islamic finance can sometimes be simply replicating non-Islamic financial policies and procedures but dressing them up in an Islamic guise.

The second main area of difficulty in Islamic financing is the myth that this sector is insulated from world economic downturns. In fact, since the world financial crisis took hold in late 2008, there have been some very significant crises within the Islamic finance sector as well. Chief among these was the Dubai debt collapse in 2009 associated with a $3.5 billion bond deal involving Nakheel, the United Arab Emirates' property developer. Uncertainty over payments to bond-holders of the world's biggest *sukuk*, or Islamic bond, caused the march of Islamic finance to falter for a time. The *Financial Times* reports that the Islamic finance industry "has been hit by the economic downturn, which caused several high-profile Islamic investment banks to default and restructure their operations and debt."[113]

The third area of difficulty is perhaps the most concerning. Sharia finance is potentially a vehicle for the spread of Sharia Law in its many other manifestations. In the words of Allyson Rowan Taylor of ShariahFinanceWatch.org, "The dictates about Sharia Law are not just the simple things about the ethical investments interest-free. It also is the same Sharia Law that we saw during 9/11. It's the same Sharia Law that allows beheadings … that goes against all the rights that we adhere to and love in the West."[114]

---

[112] Robin Wigglesworth, "Tawarruq loans split scholars", The Future of Islamic Finance (Financial Times Special Report), December 8, 2009. http://media.ft.com/cms/ac6257de-e2de-11de-b028-00144feab49a.pdf
[113] Robin Wigglesworth, "Islamic banks caught between two worlds", *The Financial Times*, 30 April 2010.
[114] Interview with Allyson Rowan Taylor on FoxBusiness.com, August 26, 2008. http://www.foxbusiness.com/video/index.html?playerId=videolandingpage&streamingFormat=FLASH&referralObject=3051056&referralPlaylistId=1292d14d0e3afdcf0b31500afefb92724c08f046&maven_referrer=staf

Even more compellingly, Frank Gaffney, **President of the Centre for Security Policy,** issues a shrill warning:

> we should be especially wary of the purported silver-lining to the current Wall Street crisis: the infusion of vast quantities of petro-dollars, primarily from OPEC's Saudi Arabia and other Islamist nations in the Persian Gulf. It is bad enough that these putative rescuers of our subprime-fueled liquidity debacle are buying up engines of our capital markets for pennies on the dollar. Worse yet, they are, in the process, putting themselves in a position to promote Shariah-Compliant Finance and the seditious theo-political agenda it serves.[115]

Lest one think that such concerns are merely the statements of Islamophobes, it is worth taking note of Muslim voices opposed to Sharia, such as the group of activists who gather under the name of Muslims Against Sharia. Their website does not mince its words: "Sharia Law must be abolished, because it is incompatible with norms of modern society."[116]

These statements state overtly what is rarely mentioned by those promoting Islamic finance; namely, that this sector is merely the tip of the Sharia Law iceberg.

---

[115] "Into the Fire", September 15, 2008.
http://www.centerforsecuritypolicy.org/Modules/NewsManager/ShowSectionNews.aspx?CategoryID=140&SubCategoryID=141&NewsID=17572

[116] http://www.reformislam.org/ (7 October 2008).

The Israel/ Palestine Conflict[117]

Martin Pakula[118]

The Israel/ Palestine conflict is part of a wider Middle East instability that threatens to erupt into a world wide conflagration. This article will be brief for so vast a subject. I will give a brief overview of recent history behind the conflict and of some of the key issues in the conflict.

History Since 1993

Oslo Peace Accords

In 1993 Israel recognised the PLO, and the PLO recognised Israel.[119] The Oslo accords were signed on September 13. Gradual withdrawal by the Israelis was to result in self rule by the Palestinian Authority (PA) in the West Bank and Gaza, and the PA in turn agreed to combat terrorism. Contentious issues were temporarily put to one side. These included the status of Jerusalem, the Israeli settlements, and the Palestinian refugees.

However after Oslo the Palestinians violated the accords by increasing their acts of terrorism. The Israelis violated the accords by increasing their settlements in the West Bank and East Jerusalem.

Writers like Mark LeVine and Gabriel Tabarani believe that the Oslo process was doomed from the start. LeVine says that neither side trusted the other.[120] A minority on either side genuinely wanted peace, but "The rest of the people, including the leadership, saw the agreements either as betrayal of the cause, or as a means to

---

[117] This paper is part of a talk that was given as the Edersheim Lecture for Christian Witness to Israel in Sydney, May 10 and in Melbourne, May 11, 2011.
[118] Martin Pakula is interim pastor of Hills Bible Church, Mont Albert, Victoria.
[119] In fact the PLO had already recognised Israel in 1988.
[120] LeVine, M., *Impossible Peace: Israel/ Palestine since 1989* (Halifax, Winnipeg: Fernwood Publishing, 2009), 46.

wage war by other (diplomatic) means."[121] Michael Rydelnik and Tabarani say that the PA never wanted peace and used the peace process as a stepping stone towards defeating Israel: "the avowed goal of many was, it seems, to obtain an agreement that would be a springboard for the destruction of Israel."[122] Arafat and the PLO committed themselves to non-violence at Oslo, but the organization they led was committed to violence and to an end of Israel. But the Israelis were also to blame. They sought to maximise their settlements, and so maximise the area they would retain, and the security that would result.

The Oslo peace process is now dead.

Camp David July 2000

In July 2000 however both sides met at Camp David. The contentious issues that had been put off were addressed. Israel's prime minister Ehud Barak offered 95% of the West Bank and all of Gaza, and compensation for the 5% of the West Bank that would be kept (for security reasons). He offered to remove some settlements and to allow 100,000 refugees to return. He offered shared sovereignty over Jerusalem.

Arafat demanded the return of all refugees and that East Jerusalem be ruled by the Palestinians (with Israeli authority over Jewish religious sites). In short, he rejected Barak's offer. The right of return of refugees was a key sticking point. For the PA, Israel didn't offer enough, and for Israel, they could not offer more.

Intifada II

In September 2000, after the failed Camp David talks, Ariel Sharon visited the Temple mount. Sharon's visit seemed to many ill advised or even provocative. Nevertheless his visit was approved by PA officials beforehand. Furthermore Sharon did not do anything to offend Muslim sensibilities. However demonstrations and riots broke out in response. Thus the second Intifada began.

---

[121] Tabarani, G. G., *Israeli-Palestinian Conflict: From Balfour Promise to Bush Declaration* (Bloomington, IN: AuthorHouse, 2008), 199.
[122] Tabarani, *Israeli-Palestinian Conflict*, Rydelnik, M., Understanding the Arab-Israeli Conflict (Chicago: Moody Publishers, 2004), 203.

Intifada II was much more severe than Intifada I. It was characterised more by terrorism and suicide bombings than by rock-throwing youths. Hundreds were killed on both sides.

The "Road Map"

In 2002 US President Bush called for a Palestinian State. He also called for an end to the use of terrorism by the Palestinian side. These points constitute the "Road Map" which was agreed to by both sides in 2003. The Road Map was overseen by the quartet of the UN, the US, the EU and Russia. The PA however has been unable to stop the terrorism on their side. Their leaders believe that an attempt to do so would lead to civil war. Thus the Road Map also lies in ruins.

Since 2003...

Israel, having given up on the peace process, decided on unilateral action which would separate the Palestinian and Israeli communities. One such action was the building of the Israeli West Bank barrier. This barrier wall follows the boundaries between Israel and the West Bank in many places, but elsewhere it encroaches into Palestinian territory to surround Israeli settlements in the West Bank. The wall is very controversial. Israel erected it for security reasons. The Palestinians say that it is an illegal land grab. For example, the UN Office for the Coordination of Humanitarian Affairs estimates that 10% of the West Bank will fall on the Israeli side of the barrier. The International Court of Justice declared in 2004 that the wall violated international law.[123]

The construction of roads between settlements in the West Bank has also resulted in the loss of land to the Palestinians. There are many check points set up along these roads. This results in Palestinian territory being broken up into what LeVine calls cantons that are separated from one another. Thus a unified Palestinian territory is impossible and their economy is undermined by the restrictions which impede the flow of commerce from area to area.[124] Thus the wall not only separates Israelis and Palestinians, but also Palestinians and Palestinians. The result of this, according to Israeli

---

[123] LeVine, *Impossible Peace*, 95.
[124] LeVine, *Impossible Peace*, 93-94.

human rights organization B'Tselem was that Israel had prevented "any real possibility for the establishment of an independent, viable Palestinian state".[125]

In 2005 Israel pulled out from Gaza unilaterally. In January 2006 elections were held for the Palestinian Legislative Council and Hamas won a majority of seats. Hamas was formed in 1987 from the Palestinian Muslim Brotherhood. Hamas is viewed by many nations as a terrorist organisation. By 2007 Hamas took full control of Gaza. They and PA have been at odds with one another. So there have been now effectively three states, not just two (Israel, the PA, and Hamas). Peace remain elusive. Is that a massive understatement?

Issues

Settlements

The building of settlements in the West Bank began after the 1967 war. After 1977, when Likud came to power (the first right wing government in Israel), there was a great increase in the number of settlements in occupied land.[126]

During the Oslo years (1993-2000) Israel "massively expanded the settlements and their population".[127] LeVine cites a 2006 study that says that "40 percent of settlement land is composed of privately owned Palestinian land that has ... been 'illegally confiscated' from the owners".[128] The settlements are considered to be illegal by the International Court of Justice (2004), the EU and the general assembly of the UN. They are said to violate the fourth article of the Geneva Convention.[129] The latter concerns occupying powers transferring its civilians into the territory it occupies.

Why is Israel doing this? At its narrowest point Israel is only 9 miles across without the West Bank, and is vulnerable to an

---

[125] Quoted in LeVine, *Impossible Peace*, 91.
[126] In 1977 when the first right wing government gained power in Israel, there were 4,400 settlers living in 31 settlements. In 2001 there were 198,000 settlers in 123 settlements.
[127] LeVine, *Impossible Peace*, 9.
[128] LeVine, *Impossible Peace*, 76.
[129] Tabarani, *Israeli-Palestinian Conflict*, 312.

invading force. For strategic reasons Israel has planted settlements and roads that ensure its future security.

Settlements remain a key issue.

Refugees

In 1948 during the war of independence (and again in 1967) many Palestinians fled from their homes and became refugees. Palestinians claim that one million were driven out in 1948.[130] Some refugees were forcibly removed. For example, 60,000 were forcibly evacuated from Lydda and Ramla.[131] This was done for security reasons. Pro-Israel sources blame Arab propaganda which caused a panic that resulted in most of these refugees fleeing. An example of the latter is the flight from Haifa. The Arab Higher Committee ordered some 15,000-25,000 to leave. The Jewish leaders urged them to stay.[132]

Whether the refugees fled because of propaganda from their own side or were forcibly removed doesn't matter in the end. Such refugees have the right to return to their homes or to be compensated for their loss. UN resolution 194 states that "refugees wishing to return to their homes and live at peace with their neighbours should be permitted to do so at the earliest practicable date". It also states that "compensation should be paid for the property of those choosing not to return". I assume Israel refuses to allow refugees to return due to continued acts of terrorism which they interpret as the Palestinians refusing to "live at peace" with them.

The problem for Israel is that if they allow the return of all the Palestinian refugees (4-5 million), Israel by population would cease to be a Jewish state. The number of Arabs flooding in would forever alter Israel's composition and it would no longer be a Jewish state. Tabarani notes that the right to self determination is guaranteed in international law and should override other

---

[130] Rydelnik claims there were not one million refugees, but a maximum of 650,000 or even only 450,000 (Rydelnik, Understanding the Arab-Israeli Conflict, 169). Tabarani claims 750,000, and 400 villages depopulated (Tabarani, Israeli-Palestinian Conflict, 62-63). The numbers are still colossal either way.
[131] Tabarani, *Israeli-Palestinian Conflict*, 68.
[132] Tabarani, *Israeli-Palestinian Conflict*, 66.

considerations. Return of refugees "would negate the Jewish right to self-determination".[133]

Rydelnik and Tabarani view the peace process as a means for the PA to bring an end to the State of Israel through insisting on the right of return of refugees. "Not only Fatah but also Arab leaders and media have unabashedly admitted that the refugee issue and right of return are being used as a means to destroy Israel."[134]

There is also the problem of Jewish refugees. After 1948 many Arab countries became hostile to their Jewish citizens. In total 400,000 came to Israel from Arab countries in the first decade of Israel's existence and a further 200,000 in the decade after that. Many were forced to leave. If compensation is given to Palestinians, the same must be given to these displaced Jews. Many who left, whether willingly or not, left behind property that was appropriated by the government.

So refugees, both Palestinian and Israeli, are an issue.

Justice

Arising from the issues of settlements and refugees is the issue of justice. Edward Said says "I see no way of evading the fact that in 1948 one people displaced another, thereby committing a grave injustice."[135]

Some would argue that if Israel is going to claim that the Old Testament gives it the right to the land, then we must also apply to Israel the standards of morality and justice that are in the Old Testament. David Torrance, who is pro-Israel writes: "Israel needs continually to be reminded, in a spirit of love and humility, of the teaching of their own Scriptures about God's command to live righteously, justly, and to welcome the stranger in their midst".[136]

The Holocaust is often highlighted by pro-Israel writers. The Holocaust was horrific and totally wrong, but that does not justify Jewish people doing the wrong thing now. In fact the very opposite

---

[133] Tabarani, *Israeli-Palestinian Conflict*, 80.
[134] Tabarani, *Israeli-Palestinian Conflict*, 82.
[135] Quoted in Chapman, C., *Whose Promised Land?* (Rev. ed.; Oxford: Lion Publishing, 2002), 11.
[136] Torrance, D. W. & Taylor, G., *Israel God's Servant* (London: Paternoster, 2007), 37.

is true. The terrible suffering of Jewish people in the Holocaust should make them very reluctant to cause suffering to others.

On the other side, Palestinian terrorism is completely unacceptable. Terrorists seek to kill or injure as many civilians as possible. Israel, I believe, seeks to minimise civilian casualties. The media is completely out of line whenever it suggests that Israel's actions are terrorist-like or Nazi-like. Israel may be flawed but it is a democracy.

Elias Chacour is a Palestinian Christian who has written very movingly about his life as a Palestinian living in Israel.[137] He and his family were driven out of their village of Biram in 1947 by Israeli soldiers, who later blew up his village. Chacour is angry about what happened, but trusts in God for justice. He blesses; he does not curse. He views violent retaliation as totally wrong. He works for peace and is prepared to suffer injustice, as his own Lord did. He believes that Israel will never achieve peace as long as they use violence.

Both sides need to recognise the suffering of the other side and not claim that suffering only for themselves, thinking that their suffering justifies wrong actions against the other. In fact Colin Chapman calls on both sides to *accept* suffering.[138] Evil is overcome in this way. There is no solution for peace that will not involve some injustice and compromise to both sides. Thus peace cannot be achieved without an acceptance of suffering and loss.

This third issue of justice, on both sides, is also a key issue.

Islam and anti-Semitism

A fourth, but more minor issue, is that of Islam and anti-Semitism.

Israel is seen as holding a Muslim land, which can never be lost and therefore must be won back. Once a land is under Muslim control it can never be allowed to pass under non-Muslim authority. Hamas therefore will never agree to a peace process or compromise because they are under the Quran as their authority. This is not the case with the PLO. During the Oslo years the differing views of Hamas and Fatah divided the Palestinians. Hamas is popular with

---

[137] Chacour, E. & Hazard, D., *Blood Brothers* (Grand Rapids, Michigan: Chosen Books, 1984).
[138] Chapman, *Whose Promised Land?*, 221-226.

the Palestinians for their good charity and social work among them. Their popularity resulted in their election victory in 2006 and mid-2008. They have used their budget to improve social services. There is far less corruption than in the PA. They believe though in violent resistance to Israel. Terrorism is seen as legitimate. Hamas and other terrorist groups have used suicide bombings that target civilians. They have used children as young as 14 as suicide bombers, and have used ambulances to hide explosives.

Hamas are anti-Zionist and anti-Semitic. Anti-Semitism in the Middle East takes the form of Holocaust denial and anti-Semitic polemics. The latter includes use of the known forgery of the *Protocols of the Elders of Zion* and blood libels.

Can there be peace?

After the failure of the Road Map some private peace proposals have been put forward. The impasse however continues. Most would agree that both sides need to look forward and not backward. There can be endless recriminations on both sides when looking to the past. Most also agree that Israel and the Palestinians cannot solve their problems themselves. Outside help is needed, particularly from the US. The US needs to be more sympathetic to the Palestinians and less one sided in its support of Israel. They need to become a fair mediator between both sides and use their influence to bring about a real solution. Very hard compromises will be needed on both sides.

Tabarani so rightly says that: "... the substantial majority of Israelis and Palestinians recognize that their future is intertwined with the other. Most deeply desire a better future for their children and grandchildren and are willing to make substantial concessions if peace and security can be achieved."[139] But there are no easy solutions and it will take decades at best to establish peace.

The most popular solution seems to be the two state solution. I particularly like Tabarani's specific suggestions for what will need to happen for peace to be achieved. I am indebted to him for what follows. First, the refugee issue. Compensation must be given and accepted as an alternative to repatriation. Compensation will be huge – in the order of many billions of dollars. The US and the international community will have to help here. Other countries

---

[139] Tabarani, *Israeli-Palestinian Conflict*, xiii.

must be willing to take in refugees, including Australia. Compensation must also be paid by Arab countries to Jewish people who were forced to leave and lost property.

Second, the settlements issue. Some settlements will need to be dismantled. Land exchange can be given for other settlements that do not affect Palestinian life and sovereignty. The wall must come down. Third, the issue of Jerusalem. Tabarani suggests West Jerusalem as the Jewish capital, and East Jerusalem as the Palestinian capital.

The main enemy to peace according to Chapman is fundamentalism. I think he is right. But he isn't just talking about Islamic fundamentalism, but any fundamentalism, including Christian and Jewish fundamentalism. The problem with fundamentalism is that such people are so ideologically driven that they cannot hear what the other side is saying and are completely and implacably one-sided. This means that a real conversation or negotiation cannot take place.[140]

So, can peace be achieved politically this side of heaven? I think so. There are examples throughout history. In the end, the cross alone is what can bring real peace: peace with God and peace with one another. There are great examples of brothers and sisters in Christ from both sides who are reconciled in Christ. Jews and Arabs will achieve this peace, when they hear the gospel and accept Jesus as their Lord and Saviour, becoming one new man in Christ. May God bring peace and reconciliation to both Jew and Arab in the promised land today.

---

[140] Chapman, *Whose Promised Land?*, 304.

Death and Dying in Hinduism and Islam

Ian Schoonwater[141]

The issue of death, though a great taboo, is a reality all must face. How we approach death is shaped by our culture, but our religion also plays a significant part. The spiritual needs of patients present a challenge to medical professionals in religiously plural societies. In the Australian Public Health System, there is an increasing focus on providing holistic care that includes meeting the spiritual needs of patients. In this article I will examine how both the Hindu and Islamic faiths treat death, what each teaches about palliative care and euthanasia, and what they teach about what lies beyond death.

The Sanctity of Life

Hindu and Muslim views on death have many similarities and yet in other aspects they are poles apart. Both faiths have a strong view on the sanctity of life, and believe that life is precious and needs to be protected and preserved, but when it comes to preserving the life of one with a terminal condition, there is a conundrum.

To the Hindu the central belief of Sanatana Dharma guides the good life. This is tied to Karma. To honour these laws, life must be preserved,[142] but this is held in tension with the teaching that eventually a person's body has served its purpose. The body is like a set of clothes that the soul removes before putting on a new set.[143] The real self is the soul and its existence is eternal. The Bhagavad-Gita explains it, *"One who has taken birth is sure to die, and after death, one is sure to take birth again."* (Bhagavad-Gita 2.27)

Similarly, the Qur'an teaches that this life is temporary, and death is the transition to the next life. The Qur'an sees this life as being a test

---

[141] Rev. Ian Schoonwater is a Presbyterian minister, he serves as Chaplain to Royal Prince Alfred and Royal North Shore Hospitals and is studying for a Master of Arts in Ministry (Islam and Other Faiths) at MST.
[142] N. Nimbalkar Euthanasia: The Hindu Perspective, National Seminar on Bio Ethics 24th and 25th January 2007, 56 www.vpmthane.org extracted (25th May 2011).
[143] S. Thrane. 'Hindu End of Life', *Journal of Hospice and Palliative Nursing*, Vol 12. No.6 November/December 2010, 338.

in preparation for the life to come. Allah is the one who gives life and takes it away: *"He created death and life that he might put you to the proof and find which of you acquitted himself best. He is the mighty, the forgiving One."* (Surah 67:2) [144]

Beliefs on palliative care

In both faiths death is not seen as something to be feared. For the Hindu it is just another process, for the Muslim it is the will of Allah. The Hindu belief is that the soul goes on beyond death. The Bhagavad Gita explains *"You were never born; you will never die. You have never changed; you can never change. Unborn, eternal, immutable, immemorial, you do not die when the body dies."* (Bhagavad Gita 2:20). This gives the Hindu comfort. For the Muslim, because of the promise of paradise, death should be prepared for, but not feared.

> As for those who say, "Our Lord is God," and take the Straight Path to him, the angels will descend to them saying "Have no fear and do not grieve; but rejoice in the Paradise you have been promised." (Surah 41.30)

In Hinduism, the ultimate goal is to achieve Moksha. The Hindu longs for liberation from the cycles of incarnations. To the Hindu the most important event in their life is their death.[145] The state one dies in will impact the destination of their soul; hence there is a strong focus on the state of mind as death approaches. The Bhagavad Gita refers to it in this way: *"Whatever state of being one remembers when he quits his body...that state he will attain without fail."* (Bhagavad Gita 8.6) In providing spiritual care to a terminal Hindu patient, the focus needs to be upon ensuring their mind is filled with thoughts of God. If they can't do this, then others can chant and read aloud from Hindu scriptures engaging the sense of hearing.[146] Most hospital units can usually make provision for these needs.

There are mixed views within Hinduism about palliative care. To most Hindus being kept alive on a machine or by other aggressive

---

[144] In this article quotations from the Qur'an are taken from N.J. Dawood's translation N.J. Dawood,. (trans) *The Koran*, London, Penguin, 1990.
[145] For the Hindu, their death is a more important event than their birth. It is because their death is what will determine where their future lies. In a pastoral care context the care of a dying patient will be far more significant than the care of a new mother and her baby.
[146] Interview with Henry Dom, 'Vaisnava Hindu and Ayurvedic Approaches to caring for the Dying', in *Innovations in End-of-Life Care* extracted from http://www2.edc.org/lastacts/archives/archivesNov99/intlpersp.asp page 2 (25 May 2011).

medical intervention will be viewed as interfering with Karma and inhibiting the natural course of death, thus leading to a bad death.[147]. The desire to be alert until death is important to the Hindu, and there is often reluctance for large doses of pain relief. To some Hindus the endurance of pain is seen as having Karmic benefits.

In Islam there is a strongly held belief that only Allah decides when someone is to die.

> "God alone has knowledge of the Hour of Doom. He sends down the abundant rain and knows what every womb contains. No mortal knows what he will earn tomorrow; nor mortal knows where he will breathe his last." Surah 31:34

As part of submission to the will of Allah, death ought not be fought, but rather accepted as the overall divine plan.[148] When a Muslim is near death, friends and family ought to gather and give comfort, and remind them of Allah's mercy and forgiveness. They may recite verses from the Qur'an, give physical comfort, and encourage the dying one to recite words of remembrance and prayer. An important hope for a Muslim is that their last words be the Shahadah.[149] The Prophet taught that sick people are very close to God and their prayers are answered.[150] The dying person should also seek forgiveness and offer it.

The approach to caring for the terminally ill and the decisions about continuing or withdrawing treatment will be influenced by world views. In both faiths decisions regarding ongoing healthcare are seen as family decisions. For many Muslims, especially in Arab countries, there is a preference for Medical Practitioners to communicate with the family before the patient, especially when communicating bad news.[151] In Hinduism, the person is viewed as comprised of mind, body, soul, in the context of family, culture and environment. Thus the family has an important role in decisions regarding health care.

---

[147] Thrane,S., 338.

[148] Aziz Sheikh, 'Death and Dying-a Muslim perspective' *Journal of the Royal Society of Medicine* Vol. 91 March 1998,138.

[149] The Creed 'There is no God but Allah and Muhammad is the messenger of Allah'

[150] K. Salman and R. Zoucha, 'Considering Faith within Culture when caring for the terminally ill Muslim patient and family', *Journal of Hospice and Palliative Care Nursing*, Vol 12. No.3 May/June 2010, 160.

[151] K. Salman, 161.

Both religions value the family gathering around and remaining with the dying person. It is not uncommon to have a continual flow of visitors or large groups visiting together. This can present many challenges in acute care settings, and medical staff are sometimes frustrated by this, but it is an important factor in providing valued spiritual care to both the patient and their family.

Teaching on euthanasia[152] and suicide

In both religions, euthanasia and suicide are in general frowned upon. In Hindu teaching, the body is seen as the temple of the soul, and premature termination of life is a violation against natural law.[153] In Islam the body is viewed as belonging to Allah.

In a Hadith it is recorded "Allah may forgive every son except in the case of one who dies Mushrik (polytheist) or one who kills a believer intentionally."[154] Islam does not regard euthanasia as justifiable. Surah 17:33 states *"You shall not kill any man whom God has forbidden you to kill, except for a just cause"*. It is Allah's decision alone when a person is to die; no one can add or subtract an hour from it. [155]

In practical terms if a Muslim becomes ill they ought to seek medical care. It is highly unusual for a Muslim patient to place a 'do not resuscitate order' on their notes. It is viewed as not doing everything possible to sustain life. Nonetheless, the prolonging of life by artificial means is also not encouraged.[156]

Islam also prohibits suicide. In one Hadith (Bukhari 2:446), Abu Huraira narrated: "The Prophet said, "He who commits suicide by throttling shall keep on throttling himself in the Hell Fire (forever) and he who commits suicide by stabbing himself shall keep on

---

[152] For the purpose of this article I will be using the legal definition "the intentional termination of life by another at the explicit request of the person who wishes to die."

[153] D. Thakrar and V. Aery. 'Death and Bereavement', in D. Thakrar, (ed) *Caring for Hindu Patients* Oxford,Radcliff, 2008, 77.

[154] Reported by Abu Daoud, Ibn Hibban, and al-Hakim. extracted from http://web.youngmuslims.ca/online_library/books/the_lawful_and_prohibition_in_islam/ch4s4p11.htm (2 June 2011).

[155] Surah 16:61.

[156] In Islam it is prohibited not to provide nourishment and hydration to the dying person (Salman p 162). There have also been a number of Fatwas issued by Saudi Arabia's Grand Mufti Shaikh Abdul Aziz bin Abdullah bin Baz stating that euthanasia is unislamic and that it is against Sharia to decide the death of a person before he is actually dead.
F. Zahedi, K. Aramesh and H. Shadi, 'Euthanasia: an Islamic Ethical perspective' *Iranian Journal of Allergy, Asthma and Immunology* Vol.6 Suppl 5 February 2007, 36.

stabbing himself in the Hell-Fire." In another Hadith (Bukhari 2:445) Jundab narrated "A man was inflicted with wounds and he committed suicide, and so Allah said: My slave has caused death on himself hurriedly, so I forbid Paradise for him." It needs to be noted, however, that nowhere in the Qur'an is suicide directly prohibited.

As with many issues, opinions about euthanasia vary within Hinduism. Dharma, the guiding principle for Hinduism is open to wide interpretation, especially in terms of the duty to care for older members of one's family or community.[157] Euthanasia disrupts the timing of death and rebirth and yields bad karma. Because life is sacred euthanasia is seen as not alleviating suffering but actually exacerbating it, in this life and the next.[158] This generates bad karma for the killed soul but also for the person doing the killing because of the violation of the principle of non-violence (ahisma).[159] On the other hand, for a doctor to alleviate a person's suffering is to do a good deed and fulfill moral obligations.[160] The patient themselves may seek an early death to ensure lucidity so they can pursue the ultimate goal of liberation from the material world.[161]

Suicide in Hinduism is not seen in terms of right or wrong but rather in terms of karmic impact. Suicide is seen as creating bad karma, because it disrupts the natural cycle of death and rebirth. According to Gyan Rajhans:

> According to Hindu beliefs, if a person commits suicide, he neither goes to the hell nor the heaven, but remains in the earth consciousness as a bad spirit and wanders aimlessly till he completes his actual and allotted life time. Thereafter he goes to hell and suffers more severely. In the end he returns to the earth again to complete his previous karma and start from there once again. Suicide puts an individual's spiritual clock in reverse.[162]

An exception to this rule is *Prayopavesa*, or fasting to death. It is only acceptable in certain circumstances, such as when the body has

---

[157] S. Thane, 56.
[158] D. Thakrar, 78. In Hinduism unlike in Islam the refusal of food and hydration is permitted.
[159] N. Nimbalker, 56.
[160] N. Nimbalkar, 56.
[161] N. Nimbalkar, 57.
[162] G. Rajhans http://gyansrajhans.blogspot.com/2010/02/modern-hindu-views-of-suicide-and.html (9 June 2011).

served its purpose and it is the right time for life to end. As starving is a gradual process it allows the person time to reflect and prepare for death. Thus it originates not from despair, but from spiritual concerns.

The dying process

In both religions there is significance attached to the dying process. To the Hindu it can be an opportunity to learn new karmic lessons and move closer to Moksha. The ideal for the Hindu would be to die in old age, at the right astrological time and the right place. The Hindu would prefer to die at home on the ground, so they are closer to mother earth.

For the Muslim, death is also an important process; it is the opportunity to meet one's creator and also presents the opportunity to ask for Allah's forgiveness for sins committed. Again it is the opportunity to submit to the will of Allah. There are a number of passages that the Muslim can take encouragement from as death approaches, such as Surah 41:30 seen previously.

Muslims believe in resurrection and final judgement, and this gives them hope and removes the fear of death. The Qur'an teaches *"The angel of death, who is given charge of you, shall cause you to die, then to your Lord you will be returned."* Surah 32:11[163]

Death rites

In both religions the deceased needs to be treated with respect. There are many similarities between Hinduism and Islam on how the body is treated at death. For example, it is preferred that persons of the same gender as the deceased handle the body. For some Hindus this goes even further, in that some prefer that only Hindus handle the body.

The Muslim family, like any family, expect the deceased's body be treated with dignity and respect. Once death is formally pronounced the rites of washing with scented water, and shrouding in a seamless white cloth need to take place. The deceased will then be transported to the site of funeral prayers, led by an Imam. The deceased is then taken to the cemetery for burial. They are laid in the grave on their right side facing Mecca. It is preferred that burial

---

[163] Zahedi, 10.

takes place within 24 hours of death. In Islam cremation is prohibited.

In Hinduism, when death is imminent the family needs to be called as well as a Brahmin (priest) who can pray with the family. The Puja (last rites) may be performed by either a priest or the family. In the case of a father it is the eldest son and in the mother's case it is the youngest son. There is a desire for drops of Ganges River water to be placed in the mouth and leaves from the sacred Tulsi plant placed on them. Another tradition is that gifts for the poor be touched by the dying person to symbolise their generosity. The priest will tie a piece of sacred thread around the neck or wrist of the dying person. As in Islam there is a ritual washing of the body [164].

Unlike Islam, cremation is the traditional method of dealing with the body in Hinduism. It is viewed as the way to allow a swifter release of the soul from the body. As in Islam preference is for the body to be put to rest the same day.

The funeral itself has an important role to play in both Hinduism and Islam. In Hinduism there is to some extent a belief that the soul needs to be told that they have died. Those who are at the funeral provide guidance. In Hinduism, some funeral chants address the dead encouraging them to let go of their attachments to material things and to continue their journey to their new existence.

In Islam following the funeral service, the family will remain and make intercession for the deceased because of the belief they are being questioned by angels. A Hadith records, "When the Prophet, may Allah bless him and grant him peace, finished burying a dead person, he used to stand over him and say, 'Ask forgiveness for your brother and ask for steadfastness for him. Now he is being questioned.'"[165].

Views on life after death

In both Hinduism and Islam there is a belief that all people have a soul. In Islam there is a belief in the afterlife; the Qur'an teaches of

---

[164] D. Jootun 'Nursing with dignity. Part 7 Hinduism *Nursing Times* Vol 98 Issue 15, 38 http://www.nursingtimes.net (18 May 2011).
[165] Abu 'Amr, and it is said Abu 'Abdullah or Abu Layla, 'Uthman ibn 'Affan said, [Abu Dawud] extracted from http://www.sunnipath.com/library/Hadith/H0004P0161.aspx (9 June 2011).

the continued existence of the soul into eternity and that there is a transformed physical existence after death. This differs significantly from the Hindu teaching of reincarnation. In Hinduism the Atman (soul) will go through infinite succession and permutation, passing many lives and experiences before merging with the divine.

For Muslims their eternal future depends primarily on performing good deeds, especially the keeping of the five pillars. The Qur'an explains that Allah will judge Muslims according to their deeds, *"Those whose good deeds weigh heavy in the scales shall triumph, but those whose deeds are light shall forfeit their souls and abide in hell forever."* (Surah 23.102)

Islamic teaching on final judgement resembles that taught in Christianity. There will be a last trumpet, the dead will rise and everyone will be for paradise or hell.

There are Hadiths that speak about a place called Al-Barzakh. This is the interval between death and the resurrection. It is seen in terms of 'soul sleep' where there is no sense of time and there is also no means of communicating with the dead. Within this realm there are two states. One is the place of blessing and bounties of Allah due to one's faith and good deeds. The other is a realm of punishment. At death the deceased is questioned by two angels. The answers given determine to which realm the person goes. The questions asked are, "Who is your God?","Who is your prophet?" and "What is your faith?"

To the Hindu, one's hope is for a better rebirth, as the attaining of Moksha is seen as almost impossible, although it is promised by Krishna in the Gita. The Hindu view on the judgement of a person's soul has some similarities to that in Islam. The Kaushitaki Upanishad (1.2-6) explains it in this way;

> "the souls of the dead ascend to the moon which is the door of heaven; there they are questioned as to their identity and if they give a wrong answer, that is, if they fail to realize their identity with Brahman, they are condemned to further empirical existence in human, animal, bird, fish or reptile form 'according to their Karma, according to their knowledge.'[166]

The deeds of a person's life will influence whether one's soul continues to the cycle of rebirth or becomes one with Brahman.

---

[166] R.C. Zahner. *Hinduism*, Oxford, Oxford University Press, 1962, 60.

Both Muslims and Hindus are reluctant to conduct autopsies. In Islam the body is sacred whether dead or alive. Thus cutting, mutilating or tampering with it in any way is considered haram.[167] This is because the soul remains in the body for a period following death. A second factor is the desire that in Hinduism the body be cremated and in Islam the body be buried as soon as possible following death.

Conclusion

Although Islam and Hinduism differ greatly both in worldview and particularly in their view of God, when it comes to death there are many similarities. These include care for the dying and respect for the deceased. That there is more to life is apparent in both Hinduism and Islam. Both also hold that the essence of a person is not just flesh and bones, but rather a person's soul, which exists beyond death. Some of these similarities can be seen in many of the world's religions.

Islam is a monotheistic religion and Hinduism is polytheistic and, both have very different views on the nature of the divine and eternity. Yet both have some strikingly similar views on judgement and the determination of a person's future particularly in relation to being questioned shortly after death.

As Australian society is changing consideration needs to be given to religious beliefs in the provision of end of life care. This presents many challenges, and at times will be almost impossible to fully implement. However, improved understanding of these needs will contribute to better holistic care practice.

---

[167] The following hadith explains this. The Messenger of Allah said: "Breaking the bone of a dead person is similar (in sin) to breaking the bone of a living person". (Sunan Abu Dawud, Sunan Ibn Majah & Musnad Ahmad).

Communiqués

Tablighi Jama'at's Ideal Woman: Invisible and Anonymous

Alan Craig[168]

She is normally a vivacious young woman. Attractive and outgoing with a touch of whacky artistic temperament, she has learnt stage magic tricks using a white dove and goldfish that endlessly surprise and entertain local children.

She is of Bangladeshi Muslim background although she has left Islam and says she has no faith. Married to a Bangladeshi Christian, they have a six year old son.

Like many others they came to the UK to free themselves from minority oppression in their home country and to make a new life. But as she sat distressed and crying in my living room, it became clear it hasn't worked out like that for them.

Four years ago she got a job as a shop assistant in a local pharmacy in the Muslim-majority area of Shadwell near their home in Tower Hamlets, east London. The shop neighbourhood is dominated by the 1,300-capacity Christian Street (sic) mosque of fundamentalist sect Tablighi Jamaat who aim to build a new headquarters mega-mosque[169] four miles further east at West Ham, close to the site of the 2012 London Olympics.

She says she gets on well with most of her customers, and with her warm friendly personality I don't doubt that's true. But soon some customers – both men with beards and women in burqas – started objecting to her western clothing. "This area is 95% Muslim," they told her, "you should cover up and wear a burqa". During the Muslim fasting month of Ramadan they objected to her enjoying a refreshing cuppa in the shop. They objected too to the non-Islamic

---

[168] Alan Craig is Leader of the Christian People's Alliance in London.
[169] http://riverinecentrenewham.co.uk/

name of her son who sometimes came to the shop after school, and to the fact that she is married to a Christian.

But her clothing was the main issue. One day early this year a man came to the pharmacy, asked her into the street outside and made it clear in no uncertain terms that she should wear a burqa. Then in April local men complained formally about her western clothing to her employer. Her response to this ongoing harassment and intimidation: "I don't want to wear Islamic clothing and in this country I'm free not to," she argued courageously, and finally reported the matter to Tower Hamlets police.

The growing Islamisation of significant areas of the UK is a complex issue. Fair-minded people will have nothing to do with Muslim-bashing. And freedom for Muslims to practice their religion is a key principle of our liberal democracy. But some Islamic values are so inimical to 21st century Britain that a challenge to them is not only inevitable, it's right.

Originating from South Asia, Tablighi Jamaat is the most successful Islamic missionary group on the planet and the UK is one of their prime missionary targets. During the recent public inquiry into the use of their West Ham site, the sect's trustees explained how they reconcile their active promotion of wedding ceremonies with the fact that theirs is a male-only mosque. At the ceremony the marriage contract is signed solely by the bridegroom and the father or brother of the bride. The bride does not sign it. She does not even attend her own wedding.

The Planning Inspector, blinded and biased by his profession's multi-cultural mores, subsequently reported merely that "the highest standards... of inclusion for women... are not being achieved" at the male-only site and that the all-male mosque is "generally an inclusive environment"! Troglodyte Saudi authorities that bar female car drivers within the regressive Kingdom can eat their hearts out: this bride-ban is happening in 21st century London apparently with the active connivance of UK authorities.

And there's yet more misogyny. One of Tablighi Jamaat's chief ideologues, Ashraf Ali Thanawi, teaches that a woman is to follow her husband's will and whims in all things, to seek his permission on all issues and to call day night if he does.[170] Another, Ashiq Elahi Bulandshahri, teaches that a woman should be confined as far as possible within her husband's home as "the devil himself begins to accompany her the moment she steps out of the house".[171] She should only be allowed out if accompanied by a male relative and concealed within a veiled black burqa.

This commodification and invisibilisation of women is alien to central Christian teaching where women, like men, are celebrated as created in the image of God. It is no surprise then that the niqab (face-veil) seems so restrictive, degrading and hostile within UK culture; one way or another in this land we are heirs to a thousand years and more of life-affirming humanity-celebrating Christianity. "If the Son sets you free, you shall be free indeed."

The pharmacy assistant is at the growing frontline clash between these value systems. "We now see more burqas in London than Dhaka," a Bangladeshi man told me recently.

Her courageous and public rejection of an imposed burqa has brought a torrent of hatred, abuse and threats around the assistant's head, and this has taken a toll on her peace of mind as I saw in my living room.

She deserves our admiration and needs our prayers.

This article first appeared in the Church of England Newspaper on Saturday, 25 June 2011.

When Some Muslims Cross the Line

Paul Nettelbeck[172]

As the New York Twin Towers of the World Trade Centre came crashing down, many Australians braced for a long night of

---

[170] http://www.amazon.com/Perfecting-Women-Maulana-Thanawis-Bihishti/dp/0520080939/ref=sr_1_1?s=books&ie=UTF8&qid=1308825298&sr=1-1
[171] http://www.darul-ishaat.co.uk/store/Twenty-Lessons-For-Muslim-Women-SKU865.html
[172] Paul Nettelbeck is based in Sydney as a tertiary education executive at Alphacrucis College (formerly Southern Cross College of the Australian Christian Churches). He is studying a double Masters degree in International Relations and Journalism at Monash University.

darkness, knowing the world had suddenly changed but wondering how. Others awoke the next morning to absolute horror and many are still trying to make sense of this dramatic clash of cultures, violently visited upon western society.

The 9/11 attack crossed the line in free and democratic societies. Ms. Sherene Hassan found her life changed more swiftly and dramatically than most. As a proud Australian and Muslim, wearing the traditional head scarf and sporting an Aussie accent, she found herself suddenly having to justify her life, not only in conversations but also through eye contact with passersby. One aggressive driver vented his road rage at the Muslim world, revving his engines, hopping and stopping as Hassan's hijab covered head crossed in front of this seething scenario.

"On September 11th 2001, I was no longer proud to be a Muslim anymore" said Ms. Hassan, living in Adelaide at that dramatic time. "I felt I was being punished for the acts of a few evil individuals". The shock jocks were firing up their audiences more than usual and being a smaller city, with fewer Muslims, Ms. Hassan had less places to hide or to blend in with a crowd.

Ms. Hassan questioned her faith after 9/11 and witnessing the loss of innocent life and how this affected her family. "My son was beside himself, he couldn't believe a Muslim would do such a thing", she says. "The Muslim teaching of respecting all living things was very much a part of our family life. My son knows that every creation of God is sacred".

A letter Ms Hassan wrote to the press to share the emotional roller coaster she was experiencing was published. "Writing that letter was very therapeutic", she says. Even more healing for Ms. Hassan, was the saddened and supportive response to her letter from a local couple. Reading their compassionate response helped her long climb out of the dark period of reflection that she found herself in. "9/11 took my life from me", said Ms. Hassan. "This response gave me my life back".

Answering a pile of supportive letters from the community allowed Ms. Hassan to connect back into mainstream life. Responding to letters written to the Muslim Women's Association of South Australia, became easier each day.

The journey for Sherene Hassan to become a proud and practicing Muslim, has been long with many twists and turns. "My father was a young Egyptian academic and my mother his tertiary student in

Iraq". In 1959 a dispute between the two countries meant that Egyptians were being asked to leave Iraq. "My mother wanted to marry her young lecturer three years her senior, much to the disagreement of her parents and homeland, so they eloped". In Morocco, they applied for Canada and Australia and were granted passage to Perth.

As a child growing up in Perth, the young Sherene distanced herself from her Muslim upbringing, not wearing any cultural or religious symbols and lying about the Christmas presents she had received, just to fit in with her mainstream Aussie friends. Ms. Hassan recalls a time in her teenage years, where she began to enjoy the communal aspects of Islam but was not yet a practicing, believing Muslim.

At University, Ms. Hassan came to Melbourne and attended a youth camp with other Muslim students. It was there she felt engaged with her cultural roots and Islamic faith with others just like herself. This is also where she met her husband and soon to be doctor Ahmed Hassan.

When questioned on the violent nature of parts of Islamic teaching and the verses in the Koran which drive some to become extremist Muslims and attack others, Ms. Hassan is quick to point out that many take these teachings out of context. "People who cross the line are similar to any people getting into cults", says Ms. Hassan.

Ms. Hassan later admits that radical Islamists have a far more sinister agenda than most people who fall into cults. "They are vulnerable for many reasons, they mostly come from secular backgrounds or are non-practicing Muslims", she concedes. "Because of the lack of contextualization, verses are misinterpreted; this occurs when vulnerable secular Muslims who have no basic foundation in religion become ultra religious overnight".

When she sees extremists speaking out, she asks "Does the Muslim community deserve crackpots like this?" and "What are we doing about it?" Around this time those questions were answered when fellow Muslim, Waleed Aly encouraged and supported her onto the board of the Islamic Council of Victoria (ICV) where she is now Vice President. The questions on violent Islam are never really answered, but instead Ms. Hassan points to detailed answers from Robert Pape on Youtube "Dying to Win". In this video, Pape suggests that suicide killings began with Jewish and Christian protesters against Roman occupation some 2000 years ago.

Pointing to these detailed answers, Hassan conveniently ignores where the modern day terrorism problem is springing from.

Ms. Hassan is also adamant that she hasn't met an extremist and that when extremists speak out, there are calls from within the Islamic community to stop them. "Any arrests of terror suspects occur due to evidence from within the community, especially within Australia", says Hassan. "When the Preston Mosque was looking for an Imam to fill in some years back, Nacer Benbrika stepped forward, speaking hatred and division in public and even worse to smaller groups of fanatics in his home".

Hassan admits to speaking to Benbrika by phone and suggests the involvement of the ICV and moderate members of the Islamic community helped secure a conviction, where he is now serving jail time for a conviction related to a plan to harm innocent fans at the MCG. To clarify what is an Islamic extremist, Hassan answers that the thousands of British Muslims calling for the death of Salman Rushdie after publishing his book 'Satanic Verses' on Islam, are indeed extreme. "Moderate Muslims wouldn't tolerate or condone that behaviour". The Salman Rushdie book is an example of a trigger that sends moderate western Muslims across the line to extremism.

Ms. Hassan admits to of up to a dozen calls to violence in the Koran but is disturbed that too many people, both radical Islamists and non-Muslims, ignore the 130 or so calls to peace. When pressed on whether these and other practices are widespread in some Islamic nations and communities, Ms. Hassan attempts to contextualize. "After each 'violent verse', immediately there is an invocation to peace". This is contrary to some objective expert opinion on the Koran, in particular referring to Surah 5:32-33 where a call to violence and murder follow after a more peaceful verse.

"Many of the (negative) practices identified with Islam are cultural and predate Islam", says Sherene Hassan as she tries to link other unidentified and isolated cases where non-Muslims are engaging in the same practices. In one case of an honour killing that occurred in Britain's Muslim community, Ms. Hassan said that these practices had also occurred in the Italian and Greek communities; however, she did not identify the specific cases.

UK House of Lords' member and global humanitarian, Baroness Caroline Cox was in Australia in 2010 and was asked about excusing extreme Islamic practices. "Pointing to prehistoric and barbaric cultural practices is no justification for the abuse of human rights for any religion or community", said the Baroness. "The freedoms to practice one's faith and enjoy protection and equality before the law in the West must be fought for in all countries", she continued. "These are Universal Declarations of Human Rights".

Baroness Cox believes that Islam will have to face its own reformation in the years ahead. She believes the academic inconsistencies of the Koran and ease by which Muslims can violently interpret teachings that advocate murder, breach human rights and endanger Islamic and western societies need to be addressed by Muslims and the global community.

Conference Reports

Symposium: What's Happening in the Middle East

The turmoil in the Middle East that has preoccupied news outlets for the last several months seems to know no end. It is like a bushfire, raging in one location for a time then jumping to another. In the process, human suffering is intense as the various authorities struggle to re-establish order, often through brutal means. As we go to press, Libya's Colonel Gaddafi has just been overthrown, while Syria and Yemen are tottering on the brink, with their respective dictators refusing to take the path of abdication as happened earlier in Tunisia and Egypt.

These fast moving events are difficult to follow for specialists, let alone for members of the public. In recognition of this, the Centre for the Study of Islam and Other Faiths (CSIOF) held a public symposium on March 22 last, entitled "What's happening in the Middle East". The purpose of the evening was to hold a public discussion among a group of Christian experts on the Middle East for the benefit of Melbourne churches.

Around 125 people turned up to hear the series of short presentations on various country contexts: Egypt, Syria, Iraq, Yemen, Jordan, and Bahrain, as well as several non-Arab countries (Iran, Turkey and Israel). Discussion took particular account of how Christian minority communities in these countries were being affected by the turmoil. All the speakers had considerable lived experiences in these countries, and they were able to speak with authority and insight on their chosen topics.

A CD has been produced, recording the evening's discussions. Further information can be obtained by contacting the CSIOF on csiof@mst.edu.au, tel: 03 9881 7839.

Symposium: Australia's Changing Demographic and its Implications for Christian-Muslim Relations

"Australia's Changing Demographic and its Implications for Christian-Muslim Relations" provided the focus of a very successful public symposium held by the CSIOF on 6 November 2010. This half-day event was modelled (with permission) upon a very successful symposium of the same name (though with a primary focus on Britain) held by the Centre for Islamic Studies of the London School of Theology in April 2010.

The approximately 50 participants first heard a paper by Peter Riddell on the topic "Islam in Europe: Concerns, Trends and Debates", with primary focus placed upon continental Europe. Statistics were presented on the growth of European Muslim communities, and attention also fell on Islamic lobby groups, such as the Federation of Islamic Organisations in Europe. Also considered was the ongoing debate about integration and perceived lack thereof among European Muslims.

While some evidence suggests that the most alarmist predictions about Islamic expansion in Europe are drawing on exaggerated statistics and unreliable predictions about future growth, at the same time polls of Muslims in various European locations show some concerning evidence of separatist worldviews among some European Muslims.

This paper concluded with a series of recommendations: Western Governments should take a more interventionist approach to the issue of social and demographic change; they should rethink the whole multiculturalism agenda to place a greater emphasis on social cohesion rather than separateness; and Churches should engage with these debates rather than resting on the sidelines in quietist isolation.

The second talk, entitled "The Demographic Problem facing Britain today, and the Churches Response", was delivered by Jay Smith, who is undertaking doctoral research at MST from his base in London. This paper addressed the growth of radicalism within the British Muslim community. It considered who was the best equipped to address this growing radicalism, suggesting that neither the Government, nor the media, nor academics could deal with this form of Islam, as it was authorised and motivated by a supposed 'divine text', a text which the secular world can neither understand nor confront.

The paper argued that the only group who could effectively confront this growing radicalism was the Christian Church, and concluded by identifying areas where Christians could be most effective, but are often not, due to certain theological presuppositions.

Symposium participants had a chance to peruse several book tables while they relaxed over coffee and cakes at the mid-point of the Symposium. Literature displays included the publications of Acorn Press, Deror Books and those of the CSIOF itself, featuring its annual Bulletin and the Occasional Papers in the Study of Islam.

After the break participants were treated to the third paper, in which Bernie Power presented a demographic analysis of the 340,000 Muslims in Australia. They represent only 1.7% of the national population, mostly living in Sydney or Melbourne.

The majority are working class, with only 27% involved in professional occupations. Muslims have two to three times the national rates of poverty, unemployment, imprisonment and use of public housing, suggesting a disadvantaged social and economic status. Some have become involved in violent plots against Australia, and all seventeen of those in prison under terrorism laws are Muslim. Others have excelled in business, sport, education and the media. Commentators are divided on the long-term impact of Islam on Australia.

The Symposium concluded with a panel session including the three speakers as well as the Symposium Chair, Dr Mark Durie, and Dr Moyra Dale. Mark emphasised the extent to which the Islam-West engagement in Europe and Britain can provide lessons for Australians. Moyra reminded the audience that such considerations of Christian-Muslim Relations, past and present, should take account of biblical teaching as discussions are held and policies are formulated.[173]

There was ample time for questions during all Symposium sessions, time that was put to good effect by a very engaged audience.

---

[173] Moyra's paper appears earlier in this issue of the *CSIOF Bulletin*.

Following the Symposium many participants proceeded to the BCV Dining Room for the CSIOF Annual Dinner attended by some 60 people. An Indonesian meal was served and fellowship was enjoyed, interspersed by an interview with Jay Smith and a talk by Bernie Power. Bernie spoke of two ideologically-opposed approaches to Islam taken by Christians in Australia, and called on Christians to maintain the balance by both loving and serving Muslims as people, as Christ called us to do, while simultaneously condemning and exposing the negative teaching of Islam with its inherent streams of inequality, human rights abuses and violence.

Feedback on both events via online surveys was extremely positive.

Muslim-Christian Forum: "Is the Qur'an the word of God?"

This forum was held in a church in Swanston St, Melbourne on Wed 15th Sept. About 120 people turned up. We were surprised at the large number. Only 6 or so Muslims attended. A positive tone for the evening was set by Peter Riddell who pointed out the offence to many Muslims caused by the threatened Qur'an burning in Florida, and the equally offensive proposed mosque near Ground Zero in New York. He appealed for an open and honest discussion with an attitude of respect.

Musa Ceratonio, an Australian convert to Islam, spoke for 30 minutes on the topic: "Why Muslims believe that the Qur'an is the word of God." He spoke clearly and confidently. His arguments included the commendable character of the prophet Muhammad and hence his reliability, as well as the scientific statements in the Qur'an, its lack of corruption (unlike some other religious texts), its lack of contradictions, that it is the "most read book in the world today" (although not "the most sold", which is the Bible) and that it has influenced Muslim nations in a positive way. He claimed that it is a unique book and that many people have converted to Islam. In the process he pointed out what he considered inconsistencies in the Bible and Christian belief.

Bernie Power then spoke for 30 minutes on "Is the Qur'an the word of God? A Christian response." He argued that the Qur'an was altered in its transmission from the angel Gabriel to Muhammad, from Muhammad to his listeners, and in the process of writing it down. He illustrated this from the earliest sources of the Sira (biography of Muhammad), the Hadith, and early Muslim scholars. He showed a pile of variant Arabic versions he had collected. He noted inconsistencies in the Qur'an's claims to be clear, and pure Arabic, without contradictions, by citing the Qur'an itself. He finished by listing differences between the teachings of the Qur'an and the Bible.

Musa responded in 5 minutes by discounting some of the sources that Bernie had cited, and claiming that the variant texts were simply pronunciation differences.

Thirty-five minutes of questions from the audience followed. Some of them had a polemical tone. A few were ruled out by Peter Riddell when the questioners wanted to engage in a shouting match with multiple questions. Questions to Musa included references to 'taqiyya' or lying by Muslims, the unknown letters in the Qur'an, and the place of Jihad in Islam.

Questions to Bernie related to the divine sonship of Christ, the Trinity, and the death of Christ.

The evening was lively, and both speakers with some friends continued the discussions late into the night in a nearby café. They hope to meet again on other occasions.

Quotations and Writings

Described by the *New York Times* as "Osama Bin Laden's worst nightmare", Irshad Manji is an outspoken Muslim feminist. Born in Uganda, her family moved to Canada when she was four. She currently serves as Director of the Moral Courage Project at New York University, and is also a Senior Fellow with the European Foundation for Democracy. Her hard-hitting critique of the perceived hypocrisy of conservative Islam is at its best in her international best-seller, *The Trouble with Islam Today: A Muslim's Call for Reform in Her Faith*,[174] which has been translated into over 30 languages and has been banned in many Muslim countries. Describing the book, she writes "I appreciate that every faith has its share of literalists... But what this book hammers home is that only in Islam today is literalism *mainstream*." The following excerpt is taken from an article in *The Times* of London, published in the wake of worldwide Muslim anger and demonstrations against the 2007 knighting of Salman Rushdie.

"As a Muslim, you better believe I am offended...

I am offended that every year, there are more women killed in Pakistan for allegedly violating their family's honour than there are detainees at Guantanamo Bay. Muslims have rightly denounced the mistreatment of Guantanamo prisoners. But where is our outrage over the murder of many more Muslims at the hands of our own?

I am offended that in April [2007], mullahs at an extreme mosque in Pakistan issued a fatwa against hugging... I am offended by their fatwa proclaiming that women should stay at home and remain covered at all times. I am offended that they have bullied music store owners and video vendors into closing shop. I am offended that the [Pakistan] government tiptoes around their craziness because these clerics threaten suicide attacks if confronted.

Above all, I am offended that so many other Muslims are not offended enough to demonstrate widely against God's self-appointed ambassadors. We complain to the world that Islam is

---

[174] St. Martin's Press, 2005.

being exploited by fundamentalists, yet when reckoning with the opportunity to resist their clamour en masse, we fall curiously silent. In a battle between flaming fundamentalists and mute moderates, who do you think is going to win?

… it is high time to "ban" hypocrisy under the banner of Islam. Salman Rushdie is not the problem. Muslims are."[175]

---

[175] "Salman Rushdie is not the problem. Muslims are", *Times Online*, 21 June 2007, http://www.timesonline.co.uk/tol/comment/columnists/article1967735.ece

Reviews

> Readers are invited to submit reviews of recent publications on the study of Islam and other faiths for possible inclusion in the *CSIOF Bulletin*.

Holy Books have a HISTORY: Textual Histories of the New Testament & the Qur'an

Keith E. Small, *Holy Books have a History: Textual Histories of the New Testament & the Qur'an*, (Avant Ministries, 2010, 126), ISBN: 9781450740777.

In his book entitled, *Holy Books have a History: Textual Histories of the New Testament and the Qur'an*, Keith E. Small sets about the task of outlining the histories of these two sacred texts and comparing them one to another. This book, recently published by Avant Ministries, is little more than 100 pages in length. Although this scholarly work is a condensed version of Small's PhD thesis (published as *Textual Criticism and Qur'an Manuscripts*, Lexington Books, 2011), it is surprisingly readable for those without formal knowledge of the subject, and, where applicable, is replete with photographs of Qur'anic manuscripts.

The primary aim of this work, Small states, is to look more closely at some of the basic dogmas upheld by the Muslims regarding these two holy texts – dogmas which are both reverential toward the Qur'an, and antagonistic toward the Bible. The two major Muslim claims which Small examines are (1) the Bible has been corrupted so as to be untrustworthy, and (2) the divinely dictated Qur'an has been perfectly preserved since the time of its first recitation (pp.vii-viii). Using the same probing methods of textual criticism which have been used on biblical texts for centuries, Small does the ground-breaking work of subjecting the Qur'anic texts to this same type of criticism and accountability.

While the unquestioned and lofty view of the Qur'an has kept Muslims from such careful examination of their text, and the sensitivity of the subject has deterred those from outside the Islamic community from approaching it, Small pioneers this much-neglected field of study, and does so with a surprising level of grace and objectivity. Although Keith Small is a Christian and thus necessarily proceeds from a certain position, his deft and scholarly approach to the study are indeed noteworthy. Rather than beginning with a certain set of dogmatic claims (eg. "the Bible is the enduring, inerrant word of God, thus all claims contrary to it are fundamentally false") and progressing from there, Small begins with a set of principles of textual criticism to which he then subjects both the Qur'anic and biblical texts. It is from this vantage point of clear research and evidence which Small seeks to view and compare the two textual traditions in question.

The method which Small uses is that which has been common to studies of ancient texts, (and specifically, the Bible) for centuries. He explains that the goal of textual criticism is two-fold: it is first "to establish the original text with as much precision as possible," and second, "to trace the historical development of the text" (19). Armed with these purposes, Small examines both the Qur'an and the New Testament texts with such research questions as:

What are the earliest attainable texts?, What are the nature and quantity of textual variants between manuscripts?, What do these variants reveal about the text and its historical development?, and How do the findings from the Qur'anic manuscripts compare to those of the New Testament? (pp.19-20).

A vast enterprise of a study to be sure – yet Small manages here to survey and encapsulate his findings in an incredibly concise and lucid manner.

Small, first, closely examines two sample texts – one from the Qur'an (Sura 14:35-41) and one from the New Testament (Acts 7:1-8). He then notes his findings on the various types of textual variants found in each. These included those of alternative spellings of proper names, variations of diacritical markings (in the Arabic texts only), omitted or substituted words, and scribal corrections or textual amendments. The most telling type of variant, however, was one which was found only in the Qur'anic manuscripts: that is, intentional changes to the text in order to standardize it to an official version (p.49).

From his research, Small draws several major conclusions. In comparison to one another, the most obvious difference between the texts of these two ancient traditions is the relatively normal level of textual variance among New Testament manuscripts and the impeccable uniformity among those of the Qur'an. Far from being persuaded of the miraculous nature of this phenomenon, however, Small points to several reasons why this appears to be the case. Both the evidences of intentional revisions of Quran manuscripts, and the accounts of Islamic history point to an imposed uniformity, rather than one derived organically. Textual evidences of this can be seen in the erasures of variants and revisions to match the official version. Interestingly, texts which are now being discovered which survived the purging of variant copies (the Sanaa manuscripts and the recovered original texts from certain Pamplisests) show a range of variability which mirrors that of the New Testament and other ancient texts (p.57).

While only one version of the Qur'an was retained and all others compulsorily suppressed, the New Testament was "standardized" by quite different means. Christians through the centuries have preserved as many manuscripts as possible, and have given them diligent study through textual criticism in order to uncover the most accurate and original versions as possible. The only purging forces came from outside persecution. To contrast these two methods of standardization, Small uses the word picture of vegetable produce which has been organically grown as opposed to commercially developed: the New Testament text was allowed to develop naturally, whereas the Qur'an was forcibly standardized in its early years with the suppression of variant versions ever since.

This issue of formal versus informal standardization is not the only one which Small addresses in this comparative study; it is, however, the one most emphasized and, perhaps, most valuable to present-day scholarship. Other subjects dealt with include the seven/ten standard readings of the Qur'an, the ambiguity of the early, unmarked Arabic manuscripts, the various diacritical marking systems, the role of oral tradition in preserving the text, and other finer points of comparison. While this book would not serve as a comprehensive study of the subjects addressed therein (presumably Small's greater PhD work from which it is derived would be substantially more involved), it is remarkable in its service to several purposes: it is an excellent introduction into a field of study which has previously been largely neglected; it is concise and readable enough to appeal to a much wider cross-section of readership than would have in any case ventured through a more extensive study; and lastly, its scholarship and fairness to both sides involved lends itself as a fitting gateway through which other scholars may enter and build upon its research.

Jannah Walters

Studies on Islam and Society in Southeast Asia

William R. Roff, *Studies on Islam and Society in Southeast Asia* (National University of Singapore Press, 2009, xvii + 354pp). ISBN: 978-9971694067

This work provides a valuable window into the prolific scholarly output by William Roff during his long (and continuing) academic career.

Readers are urged to take the time to read the Introduction, which provides the author's overview of his own career and his evolving scholarly context. It reveals how he was almost lost to Malay Studies because of his early interest in Burma and Buddhism. Roff unpacks for the reader the changing preoccupations and trends in the study of Islam in Southeast Asia and, as such, this short introduction is itself a valuable resource for young students of Southeast Asian studies.

Roff's career has been characterised by both longevity and breadth. He has spent over forty years of his life researching the modern history of Islam and Muslims, with particular reference to Southeast Asia and its social and intellectual history. The fifteen essays contained in this present volume were originally published between 1964 and 2009. They cover wide-ranging themes, though the connections across the themes are clear and provide a powerful coherence to the volume.

The content of the volume

The book is divided into five parts, with each part presenting three essays. Part I offers essays written in 1985, 1987 and 2007, addressing interpretative issues in historiography and methodology. They span a significant part of Roff's career, indicating his concern with core methodological issues down the years. They also take account of both Southeast Asian and broader Muslim world contexts, demonstrating Roff's wide-ranging knowledge base.

The first essay considers diverse methodological themes, including the transition from an earlier scholarly view of Southeast Asian Islam as syncretic and full of accretions to a view that allowed for it to be an equally valid expression of Islam, if distinctive in its own myriad ways. So important is this to Roff that he opens Chapter 1 with the statement: "There seems to have been an extraordinary desire on the part of Western social science observers to diminish, conceptually, the place and role of the religion and culture of Islam

... in Southeast Asian societies." (3) He goes on to scrutinize the scholarship of diverse Western scholarly predecessors, including Snouck Hurgronje, J.C. van Leur, Clifford Geertz, P.E. de Josselin de Jong and so forth. We will return to this issue later.

Chapter 3 ("Islamic movements: one or many?") is a fascinating chapter, engaging with the dilemma of how to reconcile vast Muslim diversity with unities that hold that diversity together. Roff does this by studying various Islamic militant movements across the Muslim world, as far removed as the Paderis in Sumatra, the Fara'idi movement in East Bengal and a Fulani jihad movement in Africa, in order to see to what extent they can be characterised as broadly "Wahhabi". This essay reflects the breadth of Roff's knowledge, both synchronic and diachronic, about the Islamic world.

Part II focuses in on Malaya and Singapore, with essays originally written in 1964, 1988 and 2004. One of the many aspects of the Roff legacy is the awareness of the key role of Singapore in Islamic developments in the Malay-Indonesian world. Chapter 4 provides a window into his contribution in this regard, with a superlative study of Malay-Muslim activities on the island at the close of the 19th century. This is followed in Chapter 5 by a study of a century of Islamisation in neighbouring Malaya, identifying the patterns of this Islamising process and the function of key elements such as the *ulama* and the *Sharia* courts.

Ever present in Roff's writing, and indeed in the processes he describes, is the lateral influences coming from other parts of the Muslim world. Chapter 6 takes account of this theme in its examination of changing institutional structures that produced the *ulama* in Malaysia, from the 19th century down to the present.

In Part III the three essays (written in 1970, 2002 and 2009) consider Arab world connections. Chapter 7 provides a fascinating account of the dynamics of the community of Malay and Indonesian students in Cairo in the 1920s, painting a portrait of their activities with particular reference to the periodical they produced, *Seruan Azhar*. Chapter 9 presents the volume's most recent essay, deriving from a paper delivered at the International Conference on Yemeni-Hadhramis in Southeast Asia held at the International Islamic University in Malaysia in 2005. This complements Chapter 8, both of which provide ample testimony to Roff's invaluable research into Hadhrami contributions to Southeast Asian Islam down the years.

In Part IV attention moves to Kelantan, with essays written in 1973, 1974 and 1983. A more narrow band of time (in terms of Roff's research career) is reflected in these essays, which follow three years when he lectured at the University of Malaya in Kuala Lumpur in the late 1960s. That post enabled him to pursue a rapidly developing interest in Kelantan's role in the emerging Malay Islamic identity.

Chapter 10 presents a valuable study of the early 20th century history of the Majlis Agama Kelantan, which provided a model for development of Majlis Agama bodies in other parts of Malaya. Chapter 12 is much more focused, dealing with debates in Kelantan about the status of the saliva of dogs. Roff describes this chapter as "a case study of conflict over authority, tribunal, and decision in Malay Islam" (250). The photo on the front cover of this book features the very Dalmatian dog that was the trigger to the dispute, which divided Kelantanese society for a time in the 1930s and which also involved Malaya's transnational Islamic connections when the dispute was referred for adjudication to the Shaykh al-Islam at Al-Azhar in Cairo.

Part V concludes the volume with essays written in 2002, 1982 and 1975 (in order of volume presentation). The three essays all consider issues connected with the Muslim pilgrimage, the *Hajj*, such as the methodology of studying the pilgrimage ritual, as well as practical matters to do with sanitation and security and specific issues connected with Malays on pilgrimage.

A Man of his Postmodern Times

Roff is clearly uncomfortable with the methodology of many earlier scholars from the colonial and immediate post-colonial periods. He subtly yet clearly criticises their "uncontrolled passion for taxonomy, an operation which, like taxidermy, is seldom best performed upon the living." (4) This is a great line, one worth remembering for dinner-party conversations. He seriously challenges Snouck Hurgronje's Islam/*adat* dichotomy; Geertz' taxonomy of *priyayi-santri-abangan* in the study of Javanese Muslims; the undefined use of terms such as "mystical", "orthodoxy", "orthoproxy" and so forth. Roff concludes his first chapter with a telling statement: "One cannot, in the interests of however desirable a patterned understanding, avoid the burden of complexity." (21)

Of course colonial scholars lived in a different age: one where traditional metanarratives reigned supreme; where colonial personnel, including scholars, often came to their tasks with a clear sense of centre and periphery, orthodoxy and heterodoxy, or simply right and wrong – an angle of approach that lent itself to taxonomies. This produced a scholarly attitude that saw certain aspects of the expressions of Islam in Southeast Asia as quaint, and interesting, but ultimately as syncretic, compared with a normative, essentialist (text-based) centre.

Such colonial scholars were men of their times. Yet Roff is equally a man of his postmodern times. Scholarship is no less subject to trend and fashion than other domain of human activity. Scholarly methods dominate for a period until they are amended, or replaced, at key hinge-points of scholarly history, when a new generation of scholars – or in some cases an outstanding individual – breaks previous moulds and sets scholarly method off in new directions.

In terms of the study of Southeast Asian Islam, Bill Roff is one of a small number of scholars who brought about such a historical hinge point of scholarly history (another is Anthony Johns, mentioned several times in this volume). They wrote in a post-World War Two context where Europeans were shedding their old metanarratives, abandoning the colonialism project (often with a sense of shame and guilt), and coming to regard the former colonial "other" as not only equally valid, but more so in many respects.

Eurocentrism came to be seen as not merely passé; it became the cause of a significant cringe factor. Postmodern Western scholarly methods did an about-face in diverse ways – one of which was to shun taxonomies, and labels and the like – because they risked creating false boundaries according to unfashionable Western perspectives of the world.

Of course, the long-held view of Southeast Asian Islam as an inferior variety to that in the Arab world was not simply imposed by Western colonial scholars. Southeast Asian Muslims themselves had long looked to the Arab world for advice, judicial opinion and conflict resolution. As Roff's essays demonstrate, Southeast Asian Muslims had long travelled to the Arab world to "top up" their expertise in the Islamic sciences, with a liberal dose added of political activism if Cairo was their destination. And in return, as Roff also demonstrates, Arab Muslims travelled to Southeast Asia, especially from the Hadhramaut, with many assuming positions of religious authority, a process no doubt helped by local perceptions of Arabs as having a special link with the context which produced the Prophet of Islam.

Even today a creeping Arabisation of Southeast Asian Islam, as a manifestation of worldwide Islamic resurgence, reflects a long-felt sense of inferiority on the part of many Southeast Asian rank-and-file Muslims, one which rightly rankles many Southeast Asian Islamic specialists.

While it is important to note Roff's caution about being too bound to taxonomies – a concern driven to no small degree by his postmodern context – we should not throw out the baby with the bathwater. Taxonomies are blunt instruments, but nevertheless they can be useful in helping us negotiate our way through a complex world – providing that they are seen as dynamic and flexible. They can, and should, be "performed upon the living."

Legacy

Bill Roff has had a profound influence on two generations of scholars of Southeast Asian Islam, both in terms of the detailed portraits he has painted of Southeast Asian Islamic societies and also in terms of advances in scholarly methodology. In time his method will be subjected to the same kind of critique as occurred (under his searching gaze) with the method of the scholarly generations which preceded him. But whatever the outcome of that process, Roff will undoubtedly be deservedly remembered as one of the greatest scholars of Southeast Asian Islamic history and society who bridged the 20th and 21st centuries.

Peter Riddell

Film Perspectives on Muhammad, from 1977 to 2011

The Life of Muhammad, dir. Faris Kermani, Crescent Films/British Broadcasting Corporation, 2011, 180 min, documentary for Television

The Message, dir. Moustapha Akkad, Filmco International Productions, 1977, 177 min, colour movie

Recent BBC documentary *The Life of Muhammad* and 1977 movie *The Message* examine the story of Muhammad, but a different flavour is given with each of their distinctive formats. Both go for three hours and follow a similar storyline, with the documentary split into three episodes (*The Seeker, Holy Wars and Holy Peace*). *The Message* has the feel of Biblical epics like *The Ten Commandments* and is well put together if a little dated 35 years on. *Life of Muhammad* is a very well produced, interesting documentary showing Islam in a positive light. *The Message* shows only the events of Muhammad's life in seventh century Arabia but *Life of Muhammad* also investigates the impact on our present world.

As a Christian who is learning about Islam, seeing this information presented on the screen brings an extra dimension. The storyline was consistent with the Muslim understanding of Muhammad's life in both programs. I felt that the BBC documentary was very positive about Muhammad's life which surprised me as they are not always so kind when presenting Christian material. Iran criticised the documentary before seeing it, believing that the "enemy" was trying to undermine Islam.[176] Unlike Salman Rushdie's book *The Satanic Verses* which Iran also condemned (examined in *Life of Muhammad*), I couldn't see anything offensive to Muslims in this documentary. When *The Message* first came out in the US, hostages were taken in three locations with demands that the film not be shown.[177] This was resolved peacefully, but it shows that it's difficult to criticise Islam because of the fear of what might happen.

In each program, we see a presentation of Muhammad's life and major events. In the beginning Muhammad received a message from God and starts to share this message with others. People start to follow him, there are fights with the polytheists and eventually Muhammad's followers triumph.

In line with Muslim tradition, neither work shows Muhammad's face, meaning he's a minor visual presence in *The Message* with others speaking and acting for him. *Life of Muhammad* discusses the initial approach to his persecutors which was to make peace, but also admits that it wasn't practical to fight with only a small number of followers in support. *The Message* dramatically portrays a small group who meet in secret and are very scared. We see the violence of the time and Muhammad's actions in the battle scenes of *The Message*. The battles are not re-enacted in *Life of Muhammad*, leaving

---

[176] http://www.guardian.co.uk/uk/2011/jun/28/iran-bbc-documentary-prophet-muhammad
[177] http://www.usatoday.com/life/people/2005-11-11-akkad-obit_x.htm

a gentler image of Muhammad. The Battle of Uhud is seen in *The Message* and most other places as a loss for the Muslims, but in *Life of Muhammad* it is described as a draw. It's not covered in detail, but this puts a different spin on Muhammad's success in battle. Though *The Message* praises Muhammad throughout, seeing the battles necessarily paints a worse picture. Despite the portrayal of Muhammad as reluctant to fight, his legacy has been a violent one, and the director of *The Message* Moustapha Akkad, was himself killed by an Al-Qaida suicide bomber in 2005[178].

In preparing these programs, the events that are ignored are as important as those included. The massacre of 900 Jewish men in Medina for alleged support of Meccan attackers in the Battle of the Ditch is missing from *The Message* but examined in *Life of Muhammad*. All men from the Qurayzah tribe were executed, while women and children were made captive, so that this Jewish tribe was exterminated. This is perhaps the only area of the documentary that gives significant coverage of the non-Muslim perspective, but it still concludes that they were killed for siding with the Meccans, not for their Jewishness. The conclusion is that there is nothing anti-Jewish in true Islam, which is at odds with both history and Islamic writings. It's easy to see why *The Message* stayed quiet on this one.

In general, the documentary presents an even more positive picture of Muhammad than *The Message*. This is partly due to the documentary format and the fact that battle scenes were not shown, only imagined. The Muslims interviewed for the BBC documentary are expected to praise Muhammad, but the non-Muslim academics included were with very few exceptions very positive too. Whether this came from editing or choice of interviewees is unclear. It's important with a documentary to be balanced, and I didn't get that impression. *Life of Muhammad* did raise some issues about Muhammad but sided with the Muslim view ultimately. In keeping with the genre of historical epics *The Message* was very positive about Muhammad, which is not a problem. Both were interesting to watch, but the BBC documentary should have explored dissenting voices at greater length.

J.S. Leslie

Postgraduate Student, MST

---

[178] http://www.usatoday.com/life/people/2005-11-11-akkad-obit_x.htm

Allah: A Christian Response

Miroslav Volf, *Allah: A Christian Response*, (New York: HarperOne, 2011), ISBN 9780061927072

Professor Miroslav Volf's new book on Allah promises to have quite an impact. The author has a significant scholarly reputation. Furthermore, the core question posed by this volume – do Christians and Muslims worship the same God – is among the most asked questions in Christian-Muslim relations today.

The volume has several strengths. It presents historical detail providing new insights into Christian-Muslim relations. The excellent second chapter considers the sequel to the 1453 disaster at Constantinople, with a discussion of Nicolas of Cusa and his thoughts on the nature of God. Then comes a consideration of Martin Luther with particular reference to his very complex views regarding Islam.

Furthermore, this volume feeds well into interfaith dialogue. The author quotes both Bible and Qur'an to show similarities in many areas, including One Creator God, a Beneficent God, Worship, the Two Great Commandments, and the Ten Commandments. At times the author also engages in apologetics in responding to Islamic viewpoints; this will equip those Christians called to that method of interaction with Muslims.

Also valuable is the author's recourse to writings by prominent Islamic scholars including al-Ghazali, al-Tabari, al-Razi, and Ibn Taymiyya. This provides some sense of an insider perspective, a crucial element in any serious study of Islam.

It is also important to acknowledge the genuine graciousness of Professor Volf, and his laudable desire to build better relations between Christians and Muslims.

However, scholarly integrity demands that some serious questions be asked about this volume. Most relate in some way to the author's methodological approach, beginning with the very first paragraph: "If for Christians Allah is a foreign and false god, all bridge building will suffer." So if Christians are serious about getting on with Muslims, they had best accept that they both worship the same God ... even before examining the evidence.

This sense of predetermining scholarly conclusions recurs at numerous points: "Muslims and Christians will be able to live in peace with one another only if ... [they] turn out to have 'a common God'" (8-9). At one point, the author issues a disclaimer: "neither Christians nor Muslims can design a God for themselves to suit the need for social harmony" (35). However, Professor Volf might be accused of having done just that.

Also questionable is the author's focus upon those Muslims and Christians "who embrace the *normative* traditions of their respective religions" (97). In a postmodernist world where so much emphasis has been placed on respecting difference and diversity, this kind of good guy/bad guy distinction based on "normativity" seems out of place. Yet we find this thread interwoven throughout the volume. We are told that "normative Islam condemns suicide as well as the killing of the innocent" (112). Normative on whose terms, one must ask. Do the suicide bombers or those who sympathise with them accept that they are not "normative"?

At times, Professor Volf's argumentation seems tendentious. Referring to Pope Benedict XVI's speech at Regensberg in 2006 which carried a reference to a statement by a medieval Byzantine emperor, Prof Volf comments that "to many hearers and readers of the pope's lecture he seemed to make the emperor's words his own." (2) A close reading of the Pope's speech shows clearly that such a perception is false. It would have helped if Prof Volf had pointed this out.

Also tendentious is his reference to the suicide bomber phenomenon: "only a miniscule fraction of 1.6 billion Muslims are suicide terrorists and only a small minority of Muslims approve of their acts" (112). No evidence is offered to support this assertion and, while the first part of the statement is likely true, the second part bears closer examination. For example, in a poll of British Muslims in 2004 one quarter of respondents indicated that Muslims should not inform on people who are involved or connected with terrorist activities. There is clearly a debate to be had here.

Another statement which serves the core argument of the book is that "Sufis ... are much more important in shaping Muslim religious sensibilities than theologians" (165). One may hope that this is correct, but how on earth does Prof Volf provide support for such a sweeping stereotype?

More broadly, the author's presentation of both Christianity and Islam throughout the volume seems designed to serve the purpose of building better relationships. Prof Volf seems to reshape Christianity to meet Muslim needs and equally to reshape Islam to work for Christians. I found myself wondering whether the Christianity being described was the faith that I adhere to, and I imagine that many Muslim readers might feel the same about the depiction of their faith. But then, this is perhaps where the concept of "normativity" tidies up the loose edges.

Also noteworthy in this volume is the selective use of Islamic textual materials. Most glaring is the sporadic reference to the important Hadith materials, only using them when they suit the book's argument. The author's brief foray into the Islam and violence connection (127) ignores the Hadith, although those who argue for a genetic link between Islam and violence draw heavily on the Hadith to argue their case. The point is that any debate cannot be engaged if key materials are set aside.

Another feature of this book is an instinctive sense of moral equivalence, reflected in a preoccupation with silencing any critical comment of Islam or Muslims with the statement that "Christians are just as bad." So on page 150 appears the trite comment that some Muslims are violent but so are some Christians. Well, obviously, but are there degrees, and if so, why so?

Similarly the discussion of "Love your enemies" (177) rationalizes Islam and Christianity as the same with an obscure and dubious reference from al-Bistami – while the author hastens to point out the sins of the crusades. Furthermore, the discussion of freedom of religion and apostasy reeks of a moral equivalence mindset, though it should be said that it concludes correctly with the statement that the issue must be based on the principle of reciprocity.

For this reviewer, the book's weaknesses lie in the expectations created for the reader by both the title and the scholarly credentials of the author. In a sense, this book is out of character for Professor Volf, who is a gifted theologian scholar. It is more a work of advocacy than scholarship. A better title for the book would have been "Improving Christian-Muslim Relations: How arguing for the same God can help". Had this reader been presented with that title at the outset, the sense of surprise at the author's shaping of the evidence to suit the core argument would not have been nearly so pronounced.

Peter Riddell

Spiders of Allah – Travels of an unbeliever on the frontline of holy war

James Hider, *Spiders of Allah – Travels of an unbeliever on the frontline of holy war* (Transworld Publishers: London, 2009, 396pp) ISBN 13:978-0-312-56585-5, ISBN – 10:0-312-56585-2.

Spiders of Allah is a journalist's overview of firsthand experience of war in Iraq, officially known (to Americans) as Operation Iraqi Freedom. However, it is not just traditional news reporting but an intricate mix of experiencing, analysing, theorising, reporting, futurrising, and philosophising on the complex situation that exists in the region in general and in Iraq in particular. The author's view of god (sic) and greed as important factors in this situation runs thread-like linking the chapters.

The book opens with a psychological analysis of the immense power gained by terrorists using Hollywood's marketing strategies. The former have done so much better than the latter. Both need and use limitless human imagination and a story in their productions. And it seems both are going to stay in business for too long. The terrorist block buster was 9/11, and since then many other low budget sequels have followed, e.g. *See Infidel Die a Horrible Death Parts I, II, and III*, posted on the internet. In true journalistic tradition, the author reports in graphic detail the blood and gore, the fear, intrigues, madness (based both on divine scriptures, and human despair of some, and on delusions of grandiosity of others). Leading up to the war were scriptural beliefs of the literalists, and myths surrounding people like Saddam Hussein believed by many to be immortal.

Iraq is the birthplace of civilizations, myths and religions.

Analyzing the events of the invasion by the West, the author argues that by the disintegration of Saddam's rule, the people were given too much freedom too soon, resulting in serious socio-politico-religious problems. Liberty and democracy were not issues to be fired up about, in areas where scurvy and dysentery were the principal concerns.

On the other side, George Bush believed God was instructing him to attack. Hider subscribes to the theory that the reason for the Iraq invasion was oil to lubricate the global economy. But he also believes that the American planners hugely underestimated the task of conquering Iraq. They thought it would be like tying a Gordian knot, but it was more like performing brain surgery. America ignored the lessons from *Histories* of Herodotus and had forgotten her own history; and had not shown enough appreciation of the long and rich history, culture and religion(s) of the region. Hence the mess.

The title of the book comes from the myths that evolved during the war. Pictures on the walls of the mosques of Fallujah declared, "Miracle of God in Fallujah". Many Iraqis believed that Allah was on their side and somehow miraculously would bring the infidels to defeat and shame. Hence the stories circulated that the bodies of the dead Muslims did not putrefy but gave out a sweet musk smell. Also, that there were ferocious camel spiders that attacked the invading infidels and killed them. Gross exaggerations about these creatures were popularized. However, the truth about them was much less exciting. While obviously dismissing such claims as untrue, Hider also raises questions about the truth of the biblical account of Gaderene swine jumping en masse into the Sea of Galilee, dismissing these and other biblical accounts as myths as well.

Hider also makes some interesting observations of the ridiculous extremes to which some Muslim fanatics went in this very chaotic time. In some areas the tomatoes and cucumbers could not be displayed together for sale, as the former could remind the buyer of female breasts and the latter of the male organ. And the bananas could only be sold in plastic bags to avoid offence. According to another report goats were to wear underpants, to avoid being a source of sexual arousal.

Hider is no friend of any religion. To him mainstream religion is the mild opiate while the fanatical fundamentalism is the distilled crack cocaine of the same stuff. "The message on the tablets was valium." Neither is he a respecter of lands. He makes sweeping observations of the human landscapes and notes that "The craziness of Middle Eastern crackpots often seems to resonate with our own homegrown variety." (324).

After masterfully leading the reader through the time- space-being tapestry of Iraq, he then looks at other important issues of the region: the Israel/Palestinian issue. Who are the Palestinians? The 1.4 million people whose homeland bears several rag tag descriptions have on one of their hills this notice: "World's largest prison camp". Hider subscribes to the theory that they are actually the descendents of the Jews that were left in Palestine at the time of the dispersal into Diaspora, and over the hundreds of years have lost their Jewish identity. He cites some interesting studies based on DNA analyses to support this theory.

The book is a clever mix of history, event-analysis, and news reporting propagating secular atheism. If the reader can stomach this hard peddling of atheism, the book is an interesting and a fair account of Iraq's war.

Akhtar Injeeli

The Third Choice: Islam, Dhimmitude and Freedom

Mark Durie, *The Third Choice: Islam, Dhimmitude and Freedom* (Deror Books, 2010, 288), ISBN 978-0-9807223-0-7 (Paperback), ISBN 978-0-9807223-1-4 (Hardback), ISBN 978-0-9807223-4-5 (Paperback, Large Print).

According to Usama Bin Ladin, "There are only three choices in Islam: either willing submission; or payment of the *jizya*, through physical though not spiritual, submission to the authority of Islam; or the sword . . ." (230) In other words, conversion, subjugation (through special taxation), or annihilation.

Pastor-scholar Mark Durie focuses on Islamic subjugation in this book. (In most lists, this comes third, not second; hence the book's title). He's well-qualified by his work on the Muslim Acehnese people of northern Sumatra, which earned him a Ph.D. from the Australian National University, a Harkness Research Fellowship for study at Leiden, MIT, UCLA, and Stanford, appointment at the University of Melbourne, and election as a Fellow of the Australian Academy of Humanities. (In the late 1990s, he moved from academia to the ministry, in which he now serves as an Anglican vicar in the Melbourne suburb of Caulfield.)

Lest one imagine that Bin Ladin's three-part standard is the product of extremist fantasy, Durie demonstrates that it is classic Islam. To do so, he cites, for instance, (1) the *Quran* at Sura 9:29, which stipulates that tribute be paid by conquered peoples (123); (2) the Sunna (the example and teaching of Mohammed) in *The Book of Jihad and Expedition*, where Mohammed lays out three options for non-believers (120); Ibn Hisham's 9th-century redaction of Ibn Ishaq's 8th century *Life of Mohammed*, which describes the prophet's dealings with conquered Jewish farmers at Khaybar (122); (4) Al-Jazeera's coverage of a *fatwa* instructing Algerian Al-Qaeda to impose the *jizya* on Christians there. (193)

Non-believers who submit to Muslim rule are called *dhimmis*, from *dhimma* (*"pact of liability"*), derived from *dhamma* (*"to blame or censure"*). (123) The premise is that these non-Muslims are the enemy, allowed to exist only on the condition that they accept demeaning and debilitating strictures. When the *dhimma* collapses because rulers find the non-Muslim populace too "uppity," *jihad* resumes -- thus the massacre of 3,000 Jews in Grenada in 1066, of 5,000 Christians in Damascus in 1860, and the Armenian genocide in Turkey before and during WWI. (157-159)

The *jizya* has amounted to as much as three month's wages (168), and has proven to be an enormous source of income for Muslim rulers. Adding insult to injury for over a millennium, a "ritual of humiliation" has often accompanied this annual collection. Typically, the official strikes the back of the payer's neck with his fist, representing potential decapitation for those "being permitted to wear their heads that year." (127, 131) Sometimes authorities drag the "infidel" to the table by a rope around his neck, shake him, pull his beard, and then cast him aside in the dust once the payment is made. (135) And, again, this is not ancient history; as late as the mid-20th century, such protocols were in effect in portions of Yemen, Iran, and Afghanistan. (139)

Traditionally, dhimmitude has extended well beyond the *jizya* -- to strictures on marriage, church repair, the wearing of crosses, travel, and the holding of public office. Dhimmis have had to build smaller homes and then quarter Muslim troops in them, ride donkeys side-saddle, surrender their seats, move out of the way on streets and sidewalk, and wear special neck rings and bells for identification. They have been radically disadvantaged in court and often consigned to "humiliating professions, such as cleaning sewers, removing dead animals, and salting the heads of executed criminals." (143-146). In 19th century Egypt, school children were taught how to curse *dhimmis*. (152) And the Nazis were not original in designing special patches for Jews to wear; Muslims had already implemented this policy, sometimes using pictures of monkeys for Jews and pigs for Christians (146), imagery taken from the *Quran*, as in 5:60.

Durie grants that maximum dhimmitude is not, at present, the official policy of any predominantly-Muslim nation, for history has not been kind to unbridled Islam; restoration of an overweening caliphate is only a Muslim dream. But gradations are everywhere to be found where elements of *Sharia* (*Quran*-based) law are entrenched or ascendant -- as in Pakistan, where the children of Muslim women and non-Muslim men are counted illegitimate (196); in Malaysia, where conversion from Islam must get court approval (197); in Egypt, where Christians are barred from Arabic studies in public universities because the *Quran* is part of the curriculum (200); in Gaza, where church bells have fallen silent. (210) And, sad to say, a form of dhimmitude has fallen on the West, as, for instance, publishers and politicians have succumbed to Muslim intimidation, offering silence, enforcing speech codes (216, 219), and even paying a form of "protection money" (213).

In exposing dhimmitude, Durie has his work cut out for him. He has to contend with the varied forms of *taqiyah* (sanctioned, strategic deception to protect or advance the cause of Islam), a flurry of myths meant to conceal the abuse (169-171) and romanticize the rule of Muslims in Spain (206), the efforts of academic enablers such as Edward Said (201-202) and a group of dialoguing Yale theologians (221), the declarations of naïve or craven politicians eager to proclaim Islam a magnificent "religion of peace" (211-213), the testimony of "dhimmi clergy" hoping to ingratiate themselves to their Muslim overseers (203-205), and the assurances or silence of *dhimmis* suffering from "battered-wife" or "Stockholm" syndrome. (184, 214)

Nevertheless, he makes his case eloquently, and with grace, as he laments the way in which Muslim cultures have injured themselves by suppressing the contribution of non-Muslims (and, of course, Muslim women). His basic introduction to Mohammed and Islam, the first half of the book, is unblinking and worth alone the price of the book. Above all, one could want no better commentary on the splendor of the Bible's instructions concerning "non-believers": "When an alien lives with you in your land, do not mistreat him. The alien living with you must be treated as one of your native-born. Love him as yourself, for you were aliens in Egypt. I am the LORD your God" (Leviticus 19:33-34 NIV).

Mark Coppenger

CSIOF News and Activities

Postgraduate Research Seminars on Islam and Related Topics 2011

Development by Muslims, with Muslims and Among Muslims: prospects and challenges
Peter Riddell, 22 March

A New Phase in the Muslim-Christian Conflict: Court battles over Church permits
Melissa Crouch, 22 March

Legends of the Fall: comparing the story of Adam and Eve in the Bible and the Koran
Mark Durie, 21 June

Can we share the gospel using Muhammad's sayings? Soteriological insights from the Hadith
Bernie Power, 21 June

Dialogue and Da'wa from Past to Present: a study of Ibn al-Layth's Risala (796AD) and Prince Ghazi's Common Word (2007)
Denis Savelyev, 23 August

Notes for Contributors

Submission requirements:

Manuscript

- Papers should not exceed 2000 words, although the Editor retains the discretion to publish papers beyond this length.
- It is preferable that submissions be prepared in Microsoft Word format.
- All papers are to be written in English, and an English transliteration given to any quotations or short phrases in original language.
- Authors are advised to use gender inclusive and non-discriminatory language.
- Any visuals should be integrated into the document, or sent separately as separate jpg or gif files with an explanation as to their position in the paper.
- Footnotes and bibliography should follow the style used in previous issues of the Bulletin.

Submission

- Papers to be considered for inclusion are to be submitted directly to the Editor.
- Submissions are to be forwarded via electronic mail to csiof@mst.edu.au. If submitting within Australia, a hard copy must also be posted to P.O. Box 6257, Vermont South VIC 3133.
- A declaration that the submitted articles are your own work and that you've acknowledged the work/s of others used in the articles in the references, etc. must be included with any submission.
- A covering letter that includes the authors' names, titles, affiliations, with complete mailing addresses, including email, telephone and facsimile numbers should be attached to the paper.

Review of submissions

- All submissions will be sent to referees for anonymous recommendation.

- The Editor holds the right to make editorial corrections to accepted submissions.

Copyright:

The CSIOF Bulletin is published by the Melbourne School of Theology Press. The copyright for any published papers will remain with the author. MST publishes these papers on the following conditions:

- They do not appear elsewhere (including web pages) for 180 days from the date of publication in the CSIOF Bulletin.
- Whenever they are printed elsewhere (including web pages), the following notice will be included: "This article first appeared in the __ issue of the *CSIOF Bulletin*".
- We retain the right to use the paper in any CSIOF publications, reprints, or in electronic form (ie. Online, CD-Rom, etc.).
- We retain the right to use a portion or description of the paper with your name in our promotional material.
- Authors are themselves responsible for obtaining permission to reproduce copyright material from other sources.
- The author will be presented with two copies of the publication.

Disclaimer:

The opinions and conclusions published in the CSIOF Bulletin are those of the authors and do not necessarily represent the views of the Editor or the CSIOF. The Bulletin serves purely as an information medium, to inform interested parties of religious trends, discussion and debates. The Bulletin does not intend in any way to actively promote hatred of any religion or its followers.

www.ingramcontent.com/pod-product-compliance
Lightning Source LLC
Chambersburg PA
CBHW051451290426
44109CB00016B/1711